METHODIST
DOCTRINE

METHODIST DOCTRINE

The Essentials

TED A. CAMPBELL

ABINGDON PRESS
NASHVILLE

METHODIST DOCTRINE: THE ESSENTIALS

Copyright © 1999 by Abingdon Press

All rights reserved.

This book is printed on recycled, acid-free, elemental-chlorine–free paper.

Library of Congress Cataloging-in-Publication Data

Campbell, Ted.
    Methodist doctrine : the essentials / Ted A. Campbell.
       p. cm.
    Includes bibliographical references.
    ISBN 0-687-03475-2 (alk. paper)
    1. Methodist Church—Doctrines. 2. Methodist Church—United States—Doctrines. I. Title.
    BX8331.2.C34   1999
    230'.7—dc21   98-43793
                                               CIP

Scripture quotations are from the New Revised Standard Version Bible, copyright © 1989, by the Division of Christian Education of the National Council of the Churches of Christ in the United States of America.

00 01 02 03 04 05 06 07 08—10 9 8 7 6 5 4 3 2

MANUFACTURED IN THE UNITED STATES OF AMERICA

To the Congregation of
Memorial United Methodist Church,
Beaumont, Texas
(1955–1983)

CONTENTS

PREFACE

It can be argued that a book on Methodist doctrine should be a short book. This one is.

Such a concise work as this can only hope to give an outline of historic Methodist teachings (see the definition of "doctrine" in the introduction). Professor Scott J. Jones is currently writing a much more substantial commentary on Methodist doctrinal statements that will complement this work for those who seek a richer understanding of our doctrinal heritage. In this little book I have tried to give accurate descriptions of historic Christian and Methodist teachings, leaving the illustration of these teachings to those who may instruct others based on this material.

Some earlier books on Methodist teachings are not well documented, and this lends the unfortunate impression that they reflect more their author's own predilections than the substance of historic Methodist teachings. While I fully own that my predilections flow through the pages following, I want to offer descriptions of historic Methodist doctrinal teachings grounded in our doctrinal sources. Even though this is a short book, documentation is important for it, because it tries to show that the material under discussion has demonstrable connections to Methodist doctrinal standards. I have used the marginal spaces both to indicate the flow of the book and to indicate references to some doctrinal sources, especially when these may be readily available to readers. Less accessible material, quotations, and the like are noted with a superscript dagger ([†]) and are documented in finer print in the "Resources and References" section at the end of the chapter in which it appears. Readers may need to refer to the glossary and index, which also include important abbreviations utilized in this book.

The first appendix contains the complete text of three doctrinal statements held in common by the AME, AMEZ, CME, and UM churches, namely, the Apostles' Creed, the Twenty-five Articles of Religion, and the General Rules.

I need to thank many persons and groups for their assistance with this project. The following individuals read initial drafts of this work and commented on them, and I acknowledge with gratitude their contributions: the Rev. Guy D. Nave, Jr., AME elder and doctoral candidate at Yale Divinity School; Bishop Thomas Hoyt of the CME Church; Professor Scott J. Jones of Perkins School of Theology, Southern Methodist University; Dr. George McClain, Executive Director, the Methodist Federation for Social Action; and Brother Jeffrey Gros, F.S.C., of the Ecumenical Secretariat of the National Council of Catholic Bishops. The combined Faith and Fellowship Class and Faithlink Class of Rockville United Methodist Church helped in reading drafts of this book in May and June of 1998. Their readings and suggestions proved to be extremely helpful in reshaping the book, and I am grateful for their assistance.

It is my prayer that Methodists will find this book helpful in learning the beliefs they hold in common with other Christians as well as distinctly Methodist emphases. In this way, I hope that their confidence in the faith may be strengthened, and that the goal of greater Christian and Methodist unity may be realized.

INTRODUCTION

METHODISTS AND DOCTRINE

This book intends to give a concise and critically accurate description of the historic teachings of four related Methodist denominations, namely,

The Intent of This Book

The African Methodist Episcopal (AME) Church,

The African Methodist Episcopal Zion (AMEZ) Church,

The Christian Methodist Episcopal (CME) Church, and

The United Methodist Church (UMC).

These four denominations share a common heritage in the Methodist Episcopal (ME) Church, which was formally organized in Baltimore in 1784. They share a common episcopal polity (a form of church government in which bishops play a central role). They share, moreover, a common set of doctrinal standards, including the Twenty-five Articles of Religion inherited from the ME Church. All of these churches had participated together in the World Methodist Council (WMC) since 1881. Through the Commission on Pan-Methodist Union, these four churches are currently engaged in a process of discernment as to the form that greater unity between them should take.

**Relation-
ships
Between
These
Churches**

It is beyond the scope of this book to give a full account of the history of divisions and reunions that led to the formation of these four churches. It might be argued that in no case did the division of these churches come about because of doctrinal differences, but this would be to take a narrow understanding of "doctrine" (see below) alien to the Methodist understanding. As we shall see, Methodist doctrinal consensus has always included consensus on moral issues. In fact, the issue of human slavery and the related issue of racial attitudes have been the most consistent factors in the division of these churches. But in order that the reader can have a cursory understanding of how these churches are related, we can summarize the following twelve steps of division and reunion:

**ME
1784**

1. The **Methodist Episcopal** (ME) Church was organized in Baltimore in 1784, and was the one church in which all four denominations in this study have roots.

**AME
late 1700s**

2. African and African American followers of Richard Allen in Philadelphia departed from the St. George's Methodist society there in 1787 because of discriminatory treatment by their fellow Methodists. They organized a society that they considered to be part of the ME Church, but continuing discrimination led them to found the Free African Society, which in turn spawned a formally separate denomination in 1816, the **African Methodist Episcopal** (AME) Church.

3. In 1796, persons of African descent in the John Street ME society in New York also formed a separate society. They were formally organized in succeeding decades as a separate denomination, the **African Methodist Episcopal Zion** (AMEZ) Church. Although we have used the abbreviation "AMEZ" in this book, the AMEZ Church is often referred to as "AME Zion" or the "Zion Methodist" Church.

AMEZ late 1700s

4. The German Reformed pastor Phillip William Otterbein in Baltimore began organizing societies in Pennsylvania and Maryland from the late 1700s. These societies were similar to the Methodist societies, although they were not formally linked to them. Otterbein's successors called themselves the **United Brethren** (UB) in Christ, and in the early decades of the 1800s they became more and more organized as a denomination.

UB late 1700s

5. A number of German-speaking Methodist societies were organized in the early 1800s by Jacob Albright. Although they were related to the ME societies in the beginning, they eventually became separate and were called the **Evangelical Association** (EA).

EA early 1800s

6. Many members of the ME church disliked the strong power of bishops in the denomination and insisted on lay representation in conferences. When their concerns were rejected, they formed the **Methodist Protestant** (MP) Church in 1830.

MP 1830

MES
1845

7. Although John Wesley and early ME conferences had ruled out slaveholding among Methodists, this moral condition for membership was increasingly neglected in southern annual conferences. The General Conference of 1844 reluctantly adopted a Plan of Separation by which the southern conferences organized in 1845 a separate church, the **Methodist Episcopal Church, South** (MES).

CME
1870

8. After the Civil War, the African American members of the MES Church formed their own denomination (1870), originally, the Colored Methodist Episcopal Church, which came to be called the **Christian Methodist Episcopal** (CME) Church.

ME+MP+
MES=
MC (1939)

9. After decades of separation, the ME, MP, and MES churches reunited in 1939 to form the **Methodist Church** (MC).

UB+EA=
EUB
(1946)

10. The UB and EA churches united in 1946 to form the **Evangelical United Brethren** (EUB) Church.

MC+EUB=
UMC
(1968)

11. The Methodist Church and the EUB Church united in 1968 to form **The United Methodist Church** (UMC).

Commissions on Pan-Methodist Cooperation and Pan-Methodist Union

12. Leaders of the AME, AMEZ, CME, and UM churches, members of the North American Section of the WMC, began meeting separately in the 1980s and formed the Commission on Pan-Methodist Cooperation, which in turn spawned the Commission on Pan-Methodist Union in the 1990s, a coalition of churches seeking to discern what forms of unity they should pursue.

Readers should note that this list does not include other Methodist churches throughout the world (such as British Methodist churches), nor even American Methodist churches beyond the predecessors of the AME, AMEZ, CME, and UM churches. The history of each constituent church in this list bears a richness and complexity that readers are encouraged to explore, but the focus of this book is on the doctrinal unity of the AME, AMEZ, CME, and UM churches.

The principal reason for the study of doctrine is so Christians can be clear about the faith they profess together. But we may note three further reasons why the study of Methodist doctrine bears particular importance now: (1) the fact that these four denominations are currently considering greater unity makes the understanding of their commonly held doctrines particularly important at this time; (2) moreover, each of these denominations requires clergy to study the doctrines of their church, but to date, these courses have not had adequate resources for the study of doctrine as corporate consensus about centrally held teachings (see the definition below) beyond works on John Wesley's theology; (3) finally, the fact that doctrine and the use of confessional statements has become a contested issue (at least in the UMC) in recent years also lends importance to the study of Methodist doctrine. The unfortunate degree of polarization within our churches calls for a careful and spiritually discerning examination of our commonly held beliefs. **Need for the Study of Methodist Doctrine**

This book takes *Methodist doctrine* to denote *that which Methodists have agreed to teach.* We **Definition of "Doctrine"** focus on consensus or agreement in teaching rather than the teachings of individual theologians. Methodist teaching has always included consensus about moral issues as well as formally "theological" issues (issues about God, salvation, the church, and so forth). However, we need to distinguish doctrine as communal or corporate agreement from *theology*, which may denote any critical reflection on religious teachings. Our scope in this book will not consider the contemporary restatement or critique of historic doctrine, but will be delimited to an attempt to describe as accurately as possible the historic consensus of Methodists on Christian teachings. Doctrine also needs to be distinguished from *popular religious beliefs* not owned as consensus through a community's established processes.

Reaching Doctrinal Consensus   Churches have utilized a variety of means by which they reach and express consensus. In the ancient church, consensus was expressed primarily through the decisions of councils of bishops. At the time of the Reformation, consensus was reached and enforced in most Protestant churches through the agency of political leadership. Only since the seventeenth century have more participatory modes of consensus developed throughout Protestant communities. Among the Pan-Methodist denominations, *Annual and General Conferences* affirm and express doctrinal consensus. General Conferences, in particular, are the only denominational bodies that can alter historic denominational doctrinal standards or add new ones that speak for the whole denomination. They also may express doctrine in less formal ways, for example, in developing new hymnals and worship resources, both of which express doctrinal consensus.

A consistent trait of the Wesleyan heritage and the Methodist churches has been a notable liberality or openness on doctrinal issues. John Wesley encouraged what he called a *catholic spirit,* a willingness to be open to, and to work closely with, those with whom he differed significantly on matters of worship and teachings not affecting the essence of Christian belief. As we shall see, Methodists have historically made very few doctrinal requirements for church membership, although they have held church members accountable for their teachings. Methodism has never claimed to be the one true church and has seldom claimed to be even the "truest" of all churches, understanding itself rather as a religious movement with a particular mission among the broader body of Christian believers. Learning the Methodist tradition should entail learning the whole of the Christian tradition in a way in which liberality or openness in doctrine is encouraged as a central spiritual discipline.

A "Catholic Spirit"

In describing his vision of a "catholic spirit," John Wesley distinguished between *essential* doctrines on which agreement or consensus is critical, and *opinions* about theology or church practices on which disagreement must be allowed. In his sermon on a "Catholic Spirit" he did not even specify what the "essential" doctrines were. But elsewhere in his writings we may discern two different sorts of essential doctrines: (a) doctrines that define the broad ecumenical or "catholic" heritage of Christian faith (these include doctrines about the Trinity, and the

"Essential" Doctrines and "Opinions"

nature of Christ defined in the early Christian centuries; doctrines about the human need for grace defined at the time of the Reformation; and doctrines about the church and its sacraments and ministries); and (b) doctrines that define the particular spirituality and teachings of the Methodist movement (especially those teachings about the "Way of Salvation" including preparatory, justifying, and sanctifying grace; see chapter 4).† That is to say, Wesley had a clear sense of that which was commonly Christian, and that which was distinctly Methodist. This sense of distinctly Methodist and broadly Christian doctrine persists in our Methodist doctrinal statements. We can see this by identifying three phases of Methodist doctrinal development.

Doctrine for a Religious Movement

The oldest Methodist doctrinal material, from the age of the Wesleys themselves, describes the distinct mission of the Methodist people. The Methodists of the Wesleys' age did not consider themselves to be a separate church, and they accepted the doctrines and the historic worship of the Church of England. The "General Rules" of the Methodist societies, Wesley's *Standard Sermons* and *Explanatory Notes upon the New Testament*, the first *Collection* of Methodist hymns, and the "Doctrinal Minutes" (utilized by the AME Church as its "Catechism on Faith") were all concerned with the working out of salvation, the role of the Methodist people as a means of God's grace, and the ethical implications of the quest for salvation. (Appendix 2 will offer more detailed notes on each of these doctrinal "standards.")

A second phase of Methodist doctrinal development came about when the Methodists became American denominations (in the period between 1784 and 1870). In this period various Methodist churches adopted doctrinal statements that express more of the fullness of Christian teaching. The Twenty-five Articles of Religion held in common by the AME, AMEZ, CME, and UM churches, as well as the UB Confession of Faith (on which the current UM Confession of Faith is based) date from this period. Both represent the inheritance of ancient and Reformation faith, and they contain very little that is distinctly Methodist. In this period, Methodist churches also had to respond to challenges from other denominations. One sign of this is the AME Church's statement on "apostolic succession," rejecting Episcopalian claims that Methodist and other churches' ordained ministries were invalid because they did not preserve an unbroken succession of bishops from the apostles. Methodist hymnals in this period also reflected the need to express the fullness of Christian teaching: in addition to teaching on the "way of salvation," for instance, they began to include more hymns in praise of the Trinity.

Doctrine for Methodist Denominations

A third phase of Methodist doctrinal development came in the last hundred years, when Methodist churches became increasingly involved in the ecumenical movement, the movement that seeks the visible unity of the divided churches ("visible" unity in addition to the invisible or spiritual unity that all Christians share) and with critical social issues, concern for which was shared ecumenically. A sign of this is the growing use by Methodists of historic Christian

Doctrine for an Ecumenical Christian community

creeds. Although Methodist churches had used the Apostles' Creed from the 1800s, they also began to utilize the Nicene Creed from the middle of the 1900s. Methodist hymnals in the last century show a consistent trend to utilize hymns from a broad variety of Christian traditions. One significant doctrinal statement from this period, the UM statement of "Our Theological Task," expresses historic Methodist teachings in the context of the "apostolic faith" shared by all Christians. Questions asked for Methodist membership also reflected the growing sense of ecumenical commitment: the UM, AMEZ, and AME churches have begun to ask candidates for church membership questions based on the baptismal creeds of the ancient church. Methodist liturgies in the twentieth century also reflect a growing identification with the broader Christian community.

Sources of Methodist Doctrine   These three phases of doctrinal development have bequeathed doctrinal statements to our churches with differing modes of formal endorsement. The four Methodist denominations whose teachings are studied here include, or refer to, some doctrinal statements in their *Disciplines* as having constitutional status (see the notes in appendix 2). In fact, we may note that the AME and AMEZ churches continue the custom of the ME church in naming their disciplinary books in a way that underscores the centrality of doctrine: *The Doctrines and Discipline of the [African] Methodist Episcopal [Zion] Church*. Among these four churches there are two doctrinal statements held in common: the Twenty-five Articles of Religion, and the

General Rules. Beyond these, the AME Church and the UMC have additional doctrinal materials. The following, then, are the nine formal doctrinal statements of the AME, AMEZ, CME, and UM churches that have been utilized in this book. Appendix 2 gives further background information on each of these documents.

1. **The Twenty-five Articles of Religion** (1784; AME, AMEZ, CME, UMC)

2. **The General Rules** (1740s; AME, AMEZ, CME, UMC)

3. **Catechism on Faith** (based on the Wesleyan "Doctrinal Minutes"; AME)

4. **Statement on "Apostolic Succession" and "Religious Formalism"** (1884; AME)

5. **Confession of Faith** (from United Brethren; 1816, and revised many times thereafter; UMC)

6. **John Wesley's** *Standard Sermons* (1700s; UMC; constitutional status in other churches is unclear)

7. **John Wesley's** *Explanatory Notes upon the New Testament* (1700s; UMC; constitutional status in other churches is unclear)

8. **The Methodist Social Creed** (originally 1908, with many revisions since; CME and UMC)

9. **Statement of "Our Theological Task"** (1972, revised 1988; UMC)

See appendix 2 for more detailed notes on each of these doctrinal statements

Other Sources of Methodist Doctrine

All of these doctrinal statements have either constitutional force (protected by the constitutions of their denominations) or at least disciplinary force (specified in a published *Discipline*) in Methodist denominations. We should also make the case that hymnals and the historic creeds included in Methodist hymnals function in practice as *de facto* standards of commonly agreed upon teaching or doctrine. Moreover, we can also state that Methodist churches have approved some ecumenical documents that indicate a level of doctrinal consensus with the broader Christian community.

Methodist Hymnals

Methodist hymnals since the middle of the 1800s uniformly begin with praise of the Trinity, recalling the worship underlying the ancient ecumenical creeds. They almost uniformly have a lengthy section on the "Christian life," laying out the more distinctly Wesleyan spiritual tradition that focuses on the "way of salvation" from recognition of sin and repentance, to justification and "assurance of pardon," to sanctification and the quest for "Christian perfection." Thus the hymnal reinforces the faith taught in the Articles and Confession, as well as the distinctly Wesleyan spirituality explicated in Wesley's *Standard Sermons* (above). We should not imply, however, that every hymn included in a Methodist hymnal carries an equal weight of consensus. Many hymns have been consistently included, and these carry a greater weight in expressing historic consensus. In addition to this, we would argue, the consistent structure of hymnals (for example, beginning with the praise of the triune God) also carries some weight in interpreting doctrine.

The Thirty-nine Articles of Religion of Wesley's Church of England formally sanctioned the use of the Apostles', Nicene, and Athanasian creeds (the "Athanasian Creed" is a fifth-century creed utilized in Western churches, but was not subsequently affirmed by Methodists). Wesley, however, omitted this article in revising the Articles of Religion for the American Methodists, and in fact he omitted the creed from the communion service in his revision of the Anglican Prayer Book, *The Sunday Service of the Methodists in North America* (1784). His exclusions certainly do not indicate any objection to the doctrines of the creeds, but are significant nonetheless because they left Methodists without a formal affirmation of the historic creeds. The Articles of Religion and the UM Confession of Faith utilize the language of the Nicene Creed (fourth century A.D.) and of the "Definition of Faith" of the Council of Chalcedon (A.D. 451), so there could be little doubt that the Methodists agreed with the content of the historic creeds.

Historic Creeds

Methodist hymnals from the middle of the nineteenth century began to utilize the Apostles' Creed in worship, and it has become the customary creed recited in American Methodist churches, including the historically African American Methodist denominations (AME, AMEZ, and CME). Only in the twentieth century have American Methodists incorporated the Nicene Creed into their hymnals, and its use in worship remains relatively rare. Perhaps the most explicit affirmation of Nicene faith on the part of Methodists comes in the four Methodist denominations' formal acceptance of the *COCU Consensus*, the doctrinal basis of the proposed "Church of Christ Uniting."

Ecumenical Commitments

The mention of the *COCU Consensus* signals another extraconstitutional expression of Methodist doctrinal commitments, namely, doctrinal commitments expressed in ecumenical agreements. Methodists participated in the World Council of Churches study of *Baptism, Eucharist and Ministry* (BEM), and here signaled for the first time that Methodists, along with other Christians, might be willing to reconsider some of their traditional concerns in the light of the ecumenical community. (For example, BEM states that "baptism upon personal profession of faith is the most clearly attested pattern in the New Testament documents".)[†] In both BEM and in the *COCU Consensus* Methodist churches have signaled their willingness to consider the office of bishop as a third "order" of ministry in addition to the orders of deacons and elders, as Catholic, Orthodox, and Anglican traditions have done in the past. Methodist dialogues (some of them conducted by the World Methodist Council) with the Roman Catholic Church and other churches may also have implications for the contemporary interpretation of doctrine.

Doctrine and Church Membership

Methodists have made few doctrinal requirements for church membership, but have consistently reserved the possibility of removing church members for "dissemination of doctrine contrary to the established standards of doctrine of the Church."[†] Through the beginning of this century Methodist churches and churches of the United Brethren in Christ tradition practiced a form of preparation that they described as "probationary membership" in a local congregation (this continues in AME, AMEZ, and CME churches, but is no longer practiced in the UM Church). An individual was received temporarily and then, after training and evidence of Christian conduct, was later received as a full member of a congregation. The focus, however, was overwhelmingly on morality and spirituality rather than profession of doctrine.

In fact, only in this century have Methodists made more explicit doctrinal requirements for church membership. The ritual for reception of adult members in the 1935 MC *Hymnal* included the question, "Do you receive and profess the Christian faith as contained in the New Testament of our Lord Jesus Christ?" This doctrinally dubious question appeared at odds with the sixth Article of Religion, which asserts the unity of the testaments, so the question was revised in the 1964 MC (then UM) *Hymnal,* "Do you receive and profess the Christian faith as contained in the Scriptures of the Old and New Testaments?" At the same time, the order for the baptism of adults added the question, "Do you believe in God the Father Almighty, maker of heaven and earth; and in Jesus Christ his only Son our Lord; and in the Holy Spirit, the Lord, the giver of life?" These same questions appear in the 1957 AMEZ, 1984 AME, and 1989 UM hymnals, although in the two more recent hymnals the profession of faith in the Trinity is set as three separate questions and allows the use of the whole of the three articles of the Apostles' Creed (said with the whole congregation) as a response. The AME and AMEZ churches are clearest in their doctrinal requirements for membership, asking candidates, "Do you believe in the doctrine(s) of the Holy Scriptures as set forth in the articles of religion of the African Methodist Episcopal [Zion] Church?"[†] One could argue, then, that in this case as in the use of the historic creeds, ecumenical dialogue and contact have influenced Methodist churches to be more explicit about their doctrinal commitments. But although church members make only a minimal profession of doctrine, they still remain liable to dismissal on grounds of teaching doctrines contrary to those of the denomination, although actual cases of dismissal on doctrinal grounds have decreased in this century.

Given that our churches seldom discipline members for doctrinal matters, we might consider the more practical dimensions of doctrine and church membership. Very few people join churches today based on doctrinal commitments, but once a person has joined a church (of whatever denomination) it becomes important to know the historic teachings of that church's tradition. Candidates for church membership should know historic Christian and Methodist teachings, and they should be familiar with Methodist worship (expressed in our hymnals) and with Methodist practices (for example, our system of appointed ministry).

Doctrine and Ordained Ministry

Candidates for ordination in Methodist churches are examined on a variety of topics, including historic Christian doctrine and specific Wesleyan teachings. Beyond these general examinations, all AMEZ and UM candidates for the order of elder and UM candidates for the order of (permanent) deacon are asked the following questions before the Annual Conference:

> Have you studied the doctrines of the African Methodist Episcopal Zion Church [UM: "The United Methodist Church"]?

AMEZ and UM candidates for the order of elder are asked the following additional question:

> Will you preach and maintain them?[†]

Although "the doctrines of our church" are not specified, this question most evidently refers to the content of the constitutionally protected doctrinal standards (listed above). The CME Church simply asks of candidates for elder, "Are you willing to conform to the *Discipline* of the Church?"[†] As in the case of lay members of congregations, ordained ministers can be removed on the grounds of teaching doctrine contrary to the church's doctrinal standards, and again, there have been decreasing cases of removal on doctrinal grounds in this century.

The reader still may wonder if there is such a thing as Methodist doctrine. It is a legitimate question. Are the agreements among Methodists trivial? Are the doctrinal standards to which we have reference in this book simply things written in books without connection to the life of Methodist Christians today? We would argue the following three points: (1) We believe that there is a substantial range of agreement found in our historic doctrinal statements, contemporary Methodist hymnals and liturgy, and even our

Methodist Doctrine?

ecumenical commitments. (2) Nothing else beyond the formal doctrinal statements examined here speaks for Methodists as *corporate* groups. That is to say, Methodists may believe any number of things as individuals, but doctrinal statements adopted by communities through their own established processes can alone speak on behalf of those *communities*. (3) In our increasingly secular culture, it is important that the church clarify its central teachings. There may have been a time when churches could simply presuppose a wide range of agreement on basic Christian beliefs. If it ever existed, that time is long past and it is now time that Methodists and other Christians be clear about what they believe and teach together. Beyond these three points, I would ask the reader to consider the particular teachings addressed in this book. For example, on the doctrine of the Trinity (see chapter 2), is there not a substantial agreement between the teachings of the Articles of Religion, the UM Confession of Faith, and the hymns (including the doxology) consistently sung in Methodist congregations? This book itself aims at demonstrating the level of consensus that exists in Methodist doctrine (as we have defined it).

★   ★   ★

Doctrine and Spirituality

"Doctrines are not God," C. S. Lewis wrote in *Mere Christianity*, "they are only a kind of map. But that map is based on the experience of hundreds of people who really were in touch with God."[†] John Wesley himself stated that doctrinal orthodoxy by itself is "but a very slender part of religion."[†] We must look beyond doctrines to discern the divine mysteries to which they refer. For Methodist folk, learning doctrine has often come by singing hymns, by hearing sermons, by learning in membership classes, or by Bible study in Sunday school. In this process, we look beyond printed or spoken words to the realities to which they refer. In teaching about the Trinity, for instance, we look to the church's worship of God. In teaching about the sinful nature of humankind, we look to the ways by which God heals creation and ourselves. In considering doctrine, then, we are examining the church's collective wisdom through the generations as it relates to life in the divine presence today.

The end or goal of Methodist teaching is not the advancement of Methodism. Our heritage has been used by God for a much greater end: the coming of God's reign or kingdom. So we should pray fervently for the day when Methodism ceases to exist, for that great day when, our historic mission having been accomplished by divine grace, the Wesleyan heritage finally dissolves into the glory of the "one, holy, catholic and apostolic church." In the words of Charles Wesley, "names and sects and parties fall; thou, O Christ, art all in all!"

The End of Methodist Doctrine

Nicene Creed; Hymnals: AME (1984), no. 529; UM (1989), no. 550

Resources and References: On the definition of doctrine, cf. Ted A. Campbell, *Christian Confessions* (Louisville: Westminster John Knox Press, 1996), pp. 2-5. Some important perspectives on the issue of doctrine in American Methodism are given in Thomas Oden, *Doctrinal Standards in the Wesleyan Tradition* (Grand Rapids, Mich.: Francis Asbury Press, 1988), Robert E. Cushman, *John Wesley's Experimental Divinity: Studies in Methodist Doctrinal Standards* (Nashville:

Kingswood Books, 1989), and William J. Abraham, *Waking from Doctrinal Amnesia: The Healing of Doctrine in The United Methodist Church* (Nashville: Abingdon Press, 1995). John Wesley's understanding of "essential" doctrine that defines the Christian community can be seen, e.g., in his "Letter to a Roman Catholic" (1748), where he rehearses the doctrines of the Nicene Creed. On the other hand the definitive doctrines of the Methodist movement are summarized in such instances as his "Principles of a Methodist Farther Explained" (1746), VI, 4-6, where he refers to the three central teachings of repentance, faith, and holiness. On the dispute over the "Wesleyan Standards," see Richard P. Heitzenrater, " 'At Full Liberty': Doctrinal Standards in Early American Methodism" in *Mirror and Memory: Reflections on Early Methodism* (Nashville: Kingswood Books, 1989), pp. 189-204; and Oden, *Doctrinal Standards in the Wesleyan Tradition* (see the reference above). On the use of the historic creeds, cf. Nolan B. Harmon, "The Creeds in American Methodism" (in *Encyclopedia of World Methodism*, s.v. "Confession of Faith," 1:563). The AME declaration on Apostolic Succession and Religious Formalism (1884) made clear that Church's commitment to the Apostles' Creed by stating that "we grant that the orderly repetition of the . . . Apostles' Creed . . . may conduce to the attainment" of spiritual worship (cited in the AME *Discipline* 1976, p. 31). The "COCU Consensus" is given in Joseph A. Burgess and Jeffrey Gros, F.S.C., eds., *Growing Consensus: Church Dialogues in the United States, 1962–1991* (Ecumenical Documents V; New York: Paulist Press, 1995, p. 42). The quotation from *Baptism, Eucharist and Ministry* is from the 1982 printing (Geneva: World

Council of Churches), p. 4. Questions asked for church membership are given in the following MC and UM hymnals: *Hymnal* of 1935, p. 543; *Hymnal* of 1964, ritual section, no. 829 and no. 828; and the *Hymnal* of 1989, p. 35. Comparable questions are asked in the AME hymnal of 1984, nos. 800 and 802, and in the AMEZ hymnal of 1957, pp. 6 and 9 of the ritual section. Lay liability to removal on grounds of teaching doctrine contrary to that of the denomination is stated in the 1996 UM *Book of Discipline,* ¶2624.3.d (p. 656). The questions traditionally asked of candidates for ordained ministry in the UMC are given in the 1996 UM *Discipline,* ¶327, questions 8-10; in the 1994 AMEZ *Discipline,* p. 79; in the 1994 CME *Discipline,* ¶420.3 (p. 110). AME candidates for ordained ministry are asked only about their fidelity to biblical teaching, although we have noted above that candidates for church membership profess fidelity to the Articles of Religion. Ordained ministers' liability for teaching doctrine contrary to that of the church is discussed in the 1996 UM *Discipline,* ¶2624, item "f." The quotation from C. S. Lewis is from *Mere Christianity* (New York: Macmillan, 1960), p. 136. John Wesley's claim that orthodoxy is "but a very slender part of religion" comes in his "Plain Account of the People Called Methodists" (1748), I:2.

CHAPTER 1

DOCTRINES ABOUT RELIGIOUS AUTHORITY

Christians need to be clear about the grounds of their teachings, but significant differences over the authority for Christian teachings have long divided the churches. Eastern Orthodox churches and the Roman Catholic Church have historically taught that the basis of all religious teaching is the unbroken unity of Scripture and later church traditions. The Protestant Reformation questioned the purity of later church traditions, and insisted on the authority of the Bible above all traditions. Since the time of the Reformation, the use of reason and reflection on common human experience (in addition to or beyond the use of Scripture and traditions) has deeply influenced Christian understandings of the grounds of religious teachings. Very often, differing understandings about the grounds of religious authority lie at the basis of other differences in Christian teaching.

The Twenty-five Articles of Religion shared by the AME, AMEZ, CME, and UM churches affirm that the Bible "containeth all things necessary to

Religious Authority

Sufficiency and Primacy of Scripture

35

Articles 5;
UM
Confession
4

salvation" (Article 5), that is, that the Scriptures teach everything that human beings need to know for their salvation. The title of this Article uses the term *"sufficiency* of the Scriptures" to describe this belief. Implied in the Articles and the UM Confession of Faith is the belief that the Bible is the *primary* source and authority for our faith, that is, no other authority can override the authority of God revealed in the Scriptures. This teaching on the primacy of the Scriptures is made explicit in the UM statement of "Our Theological Task." The Methodist teaching on the sufficiency and primacy of the Bible generally concurs with the Protestant Reformation's emphasis on the use of Scripture to reform the church. Methodists have not historically defined their understanding of the Bible's authority as involving "inerrancy" or "infallibility" of the Bible (as fundamentalist churches typically do), except that we have historically insisted that the Bible does not fail in teaching the way of salvation. Our emphasis on the sufficiency and primacy of the Scriptures does not rule out the use of Christian tradition or reflection on broader human experience (see below), but it insists that all other claims to authority must be judged by the primary authority of the Bible.

UM
"Theological
Task"

**Unity of
the Bible**

The Articles of Religion state that the Old Testament stands in continuity with the New Testament, since the one God offers salvation through Christ in both testaments (Article 6). Underlying this teaching as well as the teaching of the sufficiency and primacy of Scripture is a belief in the *unity* of the Bible, that is, the belief that the Bible tells a single story that focuses on the salvation

Articles 6;
cf. UM
Confession
4

offered through Christ. Susanna and John Wesley spoke of "the analogy of faith" that is the core message of the whole Bible telling the story of salvation.

Our historic teaching about the unity of the Bible may appear to be contradicted by more recent biblical scholarship that emphasizes the diversity of voices and perspectives in biblical literature. Methodist scholars have generally embraced this biblical scholarship, but Methodist doctrine insists that underlying the diversity of voices in the Bible is a divinely given message, at the center of which is our Savior. The UM state- UM ment of "Our Theological Task" (as revised in "Theologi-cal Task" 1988) acknowledges explicitly "a variety of diverse traditions, some of which reflect tensions in interpretation within the early Judeo-Christian heritage." But it goes on to claim that "these tra-ditions are woven together in the Bible in a man-ner that expresses the fundamental unity of God's revelation."†

The God revealed in the Bible has continued to **Tradition** act, even after the age of the apostles. *Tradition* does not mean everything that happened in the past, but *the past that we value* or treasure, espe-cially the past in which we see God's work. In affirming and valuing the past, we affirm that God's presence did not retreat after the time of the New Testament. We affirm that God has been Articles active through the history of the Christian com- 14-16; munity. We value in the past those times when we cf. AME perceived God's presence most clearly. Methodist Succession doctrine does share the Reformation's suspicion and that much in the Christian past amounted to a cor- Religious ruption of God's plan: our fourteenth, fifteenth, Formalism" and sixteenth Articles of Religion condemn teachings and practices that the Reformation judged to be corrupt. Similarly, the AME statement on "Apostolic Succession and Religious Formalism" rejects as later corruptions the teaching that all bishops must stand in an unbroken succession from the apostles, and the "formalism" that often accompanies traditional worship.

But Methodists do rejoice in God's presence in the long history of the Christian tradition: in affirming ancient creeds such as the Apostles' Creed and the Nicene Creed, we unite our voices with the voices of our Christian forebears. Our worship bears the marks of ancient and medieval Christian liturgy. Methodist hymnals now include a variety of voices from the Christian past, including texts and tunes from Catholic and Eastern Orthodox traditions, as well as from a variety of Protestant traditions. At a special called General Conference in 1970, the UMC adopted a resolution (reaffirmed in 1996) clarifying that the anti-Catholic statements in our Articles are not directed toward contemporary Catholicism or the whole of the Catholic inheritance of faith, but rather against medieval corruptions of Christian tradition, some of which were misunderstood by the Reformers. The UM statement of "Our Theological Task" affirms the critical use of Christian traditions as a source and criterion of Christian teaching.

Reason and Experience   The same UM statement affirms the use of reason and experience as sources and criteria of Christian teaching. *Reason* refers to the many ways in which human beings reflect on the world, both as individuals and as communities. John

Wesley believed that reason guided by the grace available to all persons could discern the existence of God and the need for moral responsibility; it could even illuminate the meaning of the Bible. Wesley valued *experience* especially as human contact with God, and he believed that our experience of the divine also illumined our own spiritual quest and (combined with reason) could clarify the meaning of the Bible. Wesley also believed that our experience of the material universe could teach us much, even about spiritual matters, but in every case he insisted that the use of reason and experience could not stand by themselves but had to be guided by Scripture. Reason and experience may be particularly helpful guides in relating biblical and traditional teachings to our own times, cultures, and situations.

UM "Theological Task"

In affirming the use of tradition, experience, and reason along with Scripture, the 1972 UM statement of "Our Theological Task" offered a lucid and insightful account of "Doctrinal Guidelines in The United Methodist Church." Although the statement did not attribute these four criteria as a system to John Wesley, they came very quickly to be called the "Wesleyan Quadrilateral." It has become clear since that time that although John Wesley did use Scripture, experience, reason, and the Christian past (he disliked the term "tradition"), he did not himself advocate the use of these four criteria as a method for reflection. The 1988 revision of "Our Theological Task" had to clarify that Scripture has primary authority over tradition, experience, and reason. But the "Wesleyan Quadrilateral" has proved itself as a very helpful way to call

The "Wesleyan Quadrilateral"

UM "Theological Task"

Methodists (especially United Methodists) to be clear about the grounds of their teaching, and it has proved useful as a method for ethical and practical reflection.

God's Authority and the Christian Life

Underlying Scripture, tradition, experience, and reason is the belief that God should be the guide of our lives, as communities and as individuals. We need to ask, though, whether we really value God's authority. It is one thing to speculate on the meaning of biblical passages; it is quite another thing to ask, "Do we expect to be changed by the Bible?" If we do not expect to be changed by God's revelation—in Scripture, in Christian tradition, or in reflection on our experience—then in fact we do not really own the authority of Scripture or of God known in other ways. To own the authority of God is to expect that God will challenge us, comfort us, lead us, and empower us as we discern God's message today.

Resources and References: For general comparative material on doctrines about religious authority, cf. Campbell, *Christian Confessions*, pp. 33-38 (Eastern Orthodoxy), 76-83 (Roman Catholicism), 133-44 (Reformation and Union Churches), and 205-17 (Evangelical and Free Churches). The quotation from the UM statement of "Our Theological Task" on the unity of the Bible is from the section on "Scripture" (1996 UMC *Discipline,* ¶63, p. 76). On the "Wesleyan Quadrilateral," see W. Stephen Gunter, Scott J. Jones, Ted A. Campbell, Rebekah Miles, and Randy Maddox, *Wesley and the Quadrilateral: Renewing the Conversation* (Nashville: Abingdon Press, 1997). A more critical assessment of the Quadrilateral is given in Abraham, *Waking from Doctrinal Amnesia*, pp. 56-65.

CHAPTER 2

DOCTRINES ABOUT GOD, CHRIST, AND THE HOLY SPIRIT

Historic Christianity is distinguished from other religious traditions by its worship of Jesus Christ as God. The World Council of Churches expresses this basic Christian identity when its "Basis" states that the WCC is "a fellowship of churches which accept our Lord Jesus Christ as God and Saviour."[†] In the first centuries of its life, the Christian community had to clarify this basic issue of identity, and the church's historic creeds, preeminently the Nicene Creed, reflect the church's consensus on this critical issue. The doctrine of the Trinity was the church's way of accounting for its distinctive worship of God the Father, Jesus Christ, and the Holy Spirit.

Teachings About God, Christ, the Holy Spirit

Methodist congregations regularly sing "Glory be to the Father, and to the Son, and to the Holy Ghost; as it was in the beginning, is now, and ever shall be, world without end. Amen." The doctrine of the Trinity arose out of the question of whether it was appropriate to worship Christ as God. The *Arian* teachers of the 300s A.D. claimed that Christ was divine in a sense, but was a "crea-

Doctrine of the Trinity

ture" (a created being) not to be accorded the same worship as the uncreated Father. In response to the Arians, councils of Christian bishops in A.D. 325 and A.D. 381 gave us the creed that is historically called the *Nicene Creed.* This creed clarified that Christ is "of one substance with the Father, begotten, not created" and that the Holy Spirit is "together worshipped and glorified" with the Father and the Son. Although the councils did not use the word "Trinity," they defined the trinitarian teaching that Father, Son, and Holy Spirit are equally, eternally God, together the subject of the church's adoration. The first Methodist Article of Religion and the first article of the UM Confession of Faith assert the teaching of the Trinity utilizing the language of the ancient councils, and our churches have included the Nicene Creed in Methodist hymnals since the middle of the 1900s.

The doctrine of the Trinity does not really attempt to say who God is, for the mystery of God surpasses our language and abilities of expression. The doctrine of the Trinity did set some practical limits on teaching about God. On the one hand, this doctrine maintains that we cannot so emphasize the oneness of God as to deny the personal relationships among the Father, the Son, and the Holy Spirit. On the other hand, this doctrine also maintains that we cannot so emphasize the relationships between the three divine Persons as to deny the belief that God is one.

In using language such as "Father" and "Son" about God, it was not the intention of the early

Margin notes:

Nicene Creed

Articles 1; UM Confession 1

councils to say that we must address God in exclusively masculine terms (that was not the issue). In fact, our first Article of Religion states that God is "without body or parts," and for this reason gender-specific language about God causes real problems. Some Methodists have experimented with alternative expressions for the worship of the three divine Persons, but our churches have not yet come to a consensus as to what new or revised language may faithfully express our adoration of the "three-one God" (John Wesley's favored expression) in addition to the traditional terms "Father" and "Son."

The doctrine of the Trinity made it clear that Christ is "of one being" with the Father, that Christ is fully divine. It was also important in the early Christian communities to make it clear that Christ became a true human being, and that in Christ the divine and human were perfectly united. In the words of an ancient African bishop, "Christ became human in order that humans might become divine." In the 400s A.D., a council of bishops expressed the consensus that Christ unites together a fully divine "nature" and a fully human "nature." Our Methodist Articles of Religion and the UM Confession of Faith affirm this same teaching about the "two natures" (divine and human) united in the "one Person" of Christ.

Christ as Divine and Human

Athanasius, *On the Incarnation of the Word*

Council of Chalcedon (A.D. 451)

Articles 2; UM Confession 2

One historic expression of the teaching that Christ was truly human is the statement in the Apostles' Creed that Christ "descended into hell," or "descended to the dead." This meant that Christ experienced death as fully as humans do. First Peter even states that in death Christ "went and preached to the spirits in prison," apparently

Methodist Alteration of the Apostles' Creed

Apostles' Creed

1 Peter 3:19

a reference to the belief in the early church that Christ proclaimed the good news to those who had died before the coming of the Savior. John Wesley omitted from the Methodist Articles of Religion an Anglican Article asserting Christ's descent into hell, although this probably did not indicate his disapproval. When Methodists began to include the Apostles' Creed in their hymnals in the 1800s, many did not understand the meaning of this expression. They thought that to say that Christ "descended into hell" meant that Christ went to the place of judgment ("hell," in the sense of the place of eternal punishment, see chapter 6), and so removed the expression from the creed. Growing understanding of the meaning of this expression has led some Methodist churches to include the "ecumenical" version of the Apostles' Creed, as well as the form in which Methodists have customarily said the creed.

1989 UM Hymnal, no. 882

The Holy Spirit

In defining their central teachings about Christ, early Christians had a great deal to say. They had considerably less to say about the Holy Spirit, although by A.D. 381 the Nicene Creed had been revised to make it clear that the Spirit is to be accorded equal reverence with the Father and the Son. Our fourth Article of Religion and the UM Confession of Faith affirm this teaching. These statements, however, also state that the Spirit "proceeds from the Father *and the Son*." The expression "and the Son" had been added to the Nicene Creed in the Western church in the Middle Ages, and the addition of these words to the creed was one of the issues that has divided Eastern and Western Christians since then.

Nicene Creed

Articles 4; UM Confession 3

(Eastern Christians do not believe that the bishops of Rome who authorized this change have the authority to alter the creed.) Many Protestant groups, responding to ecumenical concerns about the alteration of the creed, have elected to omit these words, and Methodist churches will need to face this issue in the near future.

Methodist piety, expressed in the UM Confession of Faith, has referred consistently to the work of the Holy Spirit in pouring out divine grace to human beings and leading us through the "way of salvation." For this reason, the 1989 *United Methodist Hymnal* places its entire section on the Christian life under the heading of the Holy Spirit. This stress on the present activity of the Holy Spirit not only characterized historic Methodist piety, but flowed from Methodism into the Holiness and Pentecostal movements.

UM Confession 3; 1989 UM Hymnal, nos. 337-536

But although Methodist piety speaks of the Spirit as the one who guides us through the way of the Christian life, we should be clear that salvation is the work of all of the Persons of the Trinity. The mystery of God is such that we cannot really divide out the works of God. So although we may speak of the first Person as the "Creator," we also recognize that "all things were made through" Christ the Word (John 1:3), and in our ordination services we pray "Come, Creator Spirit." Similarly, in the work of salvation each of the three Persons of the godhead works together on our behalf (cf. Romans 8:12-17). The Persons of the godhead cannot be reduced to functions.

What Methodist doctrine teaches about the worship of the Trinity, the nature of Christ, and the Holy Spirit is consonant with the faith of the

Methodist Emphases

Personal Nature of God

Hymnals: AME (1984), nos. 253-254; AMEZ (1957), no. 391; CME (1987), no. 112; UM (1989), no. 479

Hymnals: AME (1984), nos. 323 and 325; AMEZ (1957), no. 256; CME (1987), no. 340; UM (1989), no. 526

Love for Humankind

Hymnals: AME (1984), no. 459; UM (1989), no. 363

Hymnals: AME (1984), no. 279; CME (1987), no. 169

Worship and the Life of Faith

historic Christian community. In mentioning above the way in which Methodists have spoken of the Holy Spirit as the one who guides us in the way of salvation, though, we have identified one historic and distinctive emphasis of Methodists in teaching about God. Methodists have historically emphasized the intensely *personal* nature of God. This can be seen in Charles Wesley's hymns, for example, "Jesus, Lover of My Soul." It can also be seen in the gospel hymns favored by Methodists from the late 1800s, for instance, Fanny Crosby's "What a Friend We Have in Jesus." Although it should not be a matter of contradiction, this emphasis on the personal and relational nature of God sometimes complements the emphasis on God's objective power stressed in other Christian traditions.

Another historic Methodist emphasis has been on the *love* and compassion that God has for all humankind. With Charles Wesley we wonder, "Amazing love! How can it be that thou, my God, shouldst die for me?" And with Fanny Crosby we sing of God's compassion, "Hear the voice that entreats you, O return ye unto God! He is of great compassion and of wondrous love." Our emphasis on God's love does not contradict our belief in God's power, but Methodist devotion often stresses divine love.

When we gather to worship, we affirm as a community that which is ultimately, finally important. We meet on the first day of the week to affirm, with other Christians, that the God whom we know as the divine Trinity is the final reality. We have to live through the week in that affirmation. Luther commented on the first commandment, "That to which your heart clings and entrusts itself is, I say, really your God."[†] We face the constant temptation to cling to other things than God, to make other things, as Luther suggests, our gods. Our teaching about God grows out of our worship, where we name the true subject of our adoration: "Glory be to the Father, and to the Son, and to the Holy Spirit." *Luther's Larger Catechism*

Resources and References: For general comparative material on doctrines about God, Christ, the Holy Spirit, and the divine Trinity, cf. Campbell, *Christian Confessions*, pp. 38-47 (Eastern Orthodoxy), 83-89 (Roman Catholicism), 145-50 (Reformation and Union Churches), and 218-24 (Evangelical and Free Churches). The "Basis" of the constitution of the World Council of Churches is given in Henry Bettenson, ed., *Documents of the Christian Church* (London, Oxford, and New York: Oxford University Press, second edition, 1963), p. 333. Luther's comment on the First Commandment is from the *Larger Catechism*, given in Theodore G. Tappert, tr. and ed., *The Book of Concord: The Confessions of the Evangelical Lutheran Church* (Philadelphia: Fortress Press, 1959), p. 365.

CHAPTER 3

FOUNDATIONAL DOCTRINES ABOUT HUMAN NATURE AND SALVATION

Teachings About the Human Condition and Salvation

Historic Christian teachings about human nature and salvation attempt to describe the sinful or fallen condition of humankind and God's intention for the healing of that condition. These issues lay at the forefront of the Protestant Reformation, and many of the Methodist teachings on human nature and salvation are the inheritance of the Reformation. But John Wesley also made a distinctive contribution to understandings of salvation, especially in his attempt to understand in a methodical way what he called the "way of salvation," that is, the way in which God's intention for salvation becomes real through the life of a woman or a man. This chapter will focus on the broader, more foundational issues about human nature and salvation inherited from the Reformation; the next chapter will examine the more distinctly Wesleyan teachings about the "way of salvation."

Universal Need for Grace

Historic Methodist doctrine affirms the Reformation's passionate insistence that every human being stands in need of God's grace: we cannot possibly save ourselves. The seventh Article of

Religion states that every human being is subject to "original sin" (see below), and the eighth Article denies that human beings have any free will on their own (apart from the help or assistance of grace). These articles together make clear the belief that our salvation is the result of God's grace, not of our own work or effort.

Articles 7-8; cf. UM Confession 7; AME Catechism qqu. 15, 51-53

The presupposition of these teachings is that human beings were created in the image of God and were endowed at first with the perfect righteousness and holiness that God intended for them. Thus, the seventh Article of Religion states that original sin marks a fall from *original righteousness,* which John Wesley sometimes called "original perfection." We should note that in using the traditional Western language about *original sin,* the Methodist Article (7) affirms only that original sin denotes "the corruption of the nature of every" person. That is to say, we not only live in a world "infected" by sin, but that infection touches each of us. The Methodist Article (which Wesley edited in 1784) omits a significant phrase from the older Anglican Article stating that "in every person born into this world, [original sin] deserveth God's wrath and damnation."[†] Although Wesley's omissions do not always indicate disapproval, we know that he doubted whether God would condemn any person on the basis of original sin only.[†] As Wesley understood it, the corruption of our nature in original sin, unaided by grace, leads inevitably to "actual sin" on the part of all human beings, sin for which we are truly responsible and for which we are liable to God's judgment. But although he doubted whether original sin itself deserves con-

Original Righteousness and Original Sin

Articles 7, cf. Anglican Articles 9

demnation from God, still he believed in the universal need for grace, because he believed that every human being falls into actual sin.

Methodist Temptation to Believe in Natural Human Ability

Although historic Methodist teaching insists on the universal need for grace, there has been a tendency in Methodist teaching to deny this by claiming that human beings have "free will" or the ability to obey God's commands on their own, or by preaching as if human beings by themselves have the power to resist evil and do good.[†] Methodists have always been optimists about what grace can accomplish, and indeed have spoken of every person as having a kind of free will (see the following paragraphs). But historic Methodist teaching insisted on an optimism of divine grace (not of human effort), and insisted that humans have free will as a result of grace, not as a "natural" ability.

Universal Availability of Grace

Now (only after stating the universal need for grace) can we say what Methodists love to say about human nature and salvation, namely, that God's grace is *universally available,* that is, available to every human being. Wesley and Methodists after him rejected the doctrine of "limited atonement," the belief that only certain human beings have been elect or chosen by God for salvation and others will be damned. The teaching about limited atonement was usually associated with the belief in "predestination" as God's predetermination of who would be saved. John Wesley insisted that Christ is "the true light that enlightens every" person (John 1:9), and so Charles Wesley invited all human beings to the gospel feast: "Ye need not one be left behind, for God hath bidden all mankind" [UM: "God hath

Hymnals: AME (1984), no. 234; AMEZ (1957), no. 174; UM (1989), no. 339 (altered)

bid all humankind"]. Wesleyans reject all forms of the doctrine of predestination which imply that salvation is not possible for every human being.

This teaching set Wesley at odds with Luther, Calvin, and Augustine, in fact, with a large strain of the Western theological tradition (the "Augustinian" tradition that emphasized God's choice, election, or predestination of who would be saved). It placed Wesley and the Methodists in a rather different strain of Christian tradition alongside the broad Eastern Christian traditions, the Jesuits (among Catholics), and such Protestants as Jacob Arminius, all of whom insisted on the universal availability of grace. Because of the connection with the Dutch teacher Arminius, our teaching on universal availability of grace is sometimes described as *Arminianism*.

The "Arminian" Tradition

One implication of the Methodist's "Arminian" belief is the related belief that all human beings have *free will* to follow or reject Christ as a result of grace. Note that we say "as a result of grace": our eighth Article of Religion explicitly denies that human beings have "natural" free will ("natural" in this case means "by ourselves" or "apart from grace"). What this means, positively, is that we expect God to be at work in every human being, whether Christians, followers of other religious traditions, atheists, whomever. Methodists trust that the "free will" humans exercise, and whatever good humans may actually do, are signs that God's grace is working in them. It means, moreover, that God's initiative in salvation allows for, empowers, and requires a free human response to God's "amazing grace."

Free Will

Articles 8; UM Confession 7

The recognition of the universal need for grace

Grace and the Christian Pilgrimage

and the universal availability of grace provide a basic framework for our lives as Christians. In the next chapter we shall explore the distinctly Wesleyan form that the Christian pilgrimage may take. Here, however, we pause to note that the Christian's pilgrimage, from start to finish, is undergirded by divine grace. Our hope for healing and salvation is grounded not in our strength, but in God's. Even our hope for the sanctification of the world—for a world in which God's peace, God's justice, and God's love prevail—even this hope "is built on nothing less than Jesus' blood and righteousness" (Edward Mote).

Hymnals: AME (1984), no. 364; AMEZ (1957), no. 251; CME (1987), no. 223; UM (1989), no. 368

Resources and References: For general comparative material on doctrines about human nature and salvation, cf. Campbell, *Christian Confessions*, pp. 47-53 (Eastern Orthodoxy), 90-96 (Roman Catholicism), 150-62 (Reformation and Union churches), and 224-35 (Evangelical and Free churches). The text of the ninth Anglican Article (answering to the seventh Methodist Article) is given in Leith's *Creeds of the Churches*, pp. 269-70. Wesley's doubt about whether persons would be condemned on the basis of original sin only was expressed in a letter to John Mason, 21 November 1756 (in John Telford, ed., *Letters of the Reverend John Wesley, A.M.* ["Standard Edition" of the Works of John Wesley; 8 vols.; London: Epworth Press, 1931], 6:239-40). The tendency in Methodist theology to insist on natural human ability and free will is documented by Robert E. Chiles in *Theological Transition in American Methodism, 1790–1935* (New York and Nashville: Abingdon Press, 1965; chapter 5, "From Free Grace to Free Will," pp. 144-83).

CHAPTER 4

DISTINCTIVELY WESLEYAN DOCTRINES ABOUT THE "WAY OF SALVATION"

Building on the foundational teachings about the universal human need for grace and the universal availability of grace, John Wesley and the early Methodists became fascinated with the process by which women and men actually live out the life of grace. John Wesley sometimes referred to this process as the "way of salvation," as in the title of one of his sermons, "The Scripture Way of Salvation." Wesley considered himself to be a scientific observer of the religious life, constantly inquiring about persons' religious experience, making notes, and reaching conclusions based on his and others' experience. Teachings about the "way of salvation" express more of the distinctive spirituality of the Wesleyan movement. For that reason, this chapter will rely more on the Wesleyan sources (including John Wesley's *Sermons*) than other chapters in this book.

The pattern of Methodist teaching about the "way of salvation" has persisted consistently in Methodist hymnals. The first Methodist hymnal,

John and Charles Wesley's *Collection of Hymns for the Use of the People Called Methodists* (1780) was organized, as John Wesley noted, to show the experience of believers. Subsequent Methodist hymnals typically have a long section, often entitled "The Christian Life," in which hymns are arranged according to the "way of salvation," from repentance to faith and justification to sanctification (see below). This chapter, then, examines the distinctive Wesleyan spiritual inheritance in speaking about the "way of salvation."

Organizing the Way of Salvation

John Wesley sometimes organized his understanding of the "way of salvation" under the three headings of "preventing grace" (God's grace coming before we believe in Christ), "justifying grace" (God's grace enabling us to believe in Christ) and "sanctifying grace" (God's grace leading us to holiness).† The 1989 *United Methodist Hymnal* utilizes a similar scheme of "prevenient," justifying and sanctifying grace. The text following utilizes this scheme, although Wesley himself could develop much more elaborate descriptions of the "way of salvation" and many Methodist hymnals have more elaborate organizational schemes to describe the process of the Christian life.

Prevenient Grace

The eighth Article of Religion and the writings of John Wesley refer to God's "preventing" grace. In John Wesley's time and before, the term "preventing" meant simply "coming before" (Latin, *preveniens*). Because the meaning of the term has changed considerably, we tend to speak today of God's "prevenient" grace, as in the headings of the 1989 *United Methodist*

Articles 8

Hymnal. In either case the meaning is the same: "preventing" or "prevenient" grace means God's grace "coming before" our believing in Christ. We might speak more intelligibly by calling it "preparatory" or "assisting" grace, the latter being the term employed in the AME *Discipline* in the Articles of Religion. Consistent with the Arminian belief in the universal availability of grace, Methodists have consistently maintained that prevenient grace is God's grace given to every human being (see chapter 3). Thus, whenever any human being does good (Christian or not), we rejoice in the presence of divine grace.

Prevenient grace is the appropriate heading under which Methodists have described all the ways in which God works with human beings *before* they believe in Christ (again, "prevenient" refers to grace *coming before* faith in Christ). Prevenient grace leads us to *repentance,* sorrow over sin and the realization that we are unable to save ourselves. For many Methodists through the centuries, this came as a vivid religious experience they called "conviction" or *awakening,* the experience in which a person comes to the terrible realization of one's dangerous condition before God. For some Methodists, awakening came with intense emotional signs: crying out in terror, "mourning" or "moaning," even loss of consciousness. In Methodist camp meetings, a "mourner's bench" in front of the altar represented the place of repentance before faith. For some Methodists, the experience of prevenient grace came less as a vivid experience and more as a growing sense of the need for God. But it is important to realize that although these experi-

Repentance and "Awakening"

ences could seem dreadful, they were understood as a sign of God's work in the person. Methodists did not feel that they should hasten a person's conversion—that was God's work.

Justifying Grace

Articles 9; UM Confession 9; AME Catechism, qqu. 1-7, 70-72

Wesley, "Salvation by Faith" I:2 and 4

Prevenient grace leads to *justifying grace,* the grace of God by which, through faith in Christ, our sins are forgiven. With the Protestant Reformers, Wesley and the Methodists insisted that our justification is by grace through faith (Ephesians 2:8-10). The forgiveness of sins does not rely on goodness or merit or good works on our part. But Wesley and the Methodists insisted that faith is not simply a matter of knowing doctrines: Wesley's sermon on "Salvation by Faith" makes the point that even the devils know that Jesus is the Christ. The faith by which we are justified involves not merely knowledge about Christ; it involves heartfelt trust in Christ.

Assurance of Pardon

AME Catechism, qqu. 8, 31-39; cf. J. Wesley's Journal for 24 May 1738

The normal experience of early Methodist people involved not only belief in Christ but also a supernatural sense that one's sins had been pardoned by Christ. John Wesley and the Methodists referred to this aspect of their religious experience as "assurance of pardon." For them, assurance of pardon often came as a sense of divine peace following the tumult of "awakening" and repentance (see above). John Wesley's own experience at Aldersgate (24 May 1738) involved a divinely given "assurance."

Immediately after he had this vivid religious experience, John Wesley insisted that without assurance of pardon, there is no true justifying faith. But his continuing investigations into the religious experiences of men and women led him to recognize that the experience of assurance does not always accompany justification. Even still, he maintained that assurance was the "common privilege" of believers. Some of Charles Wesley's boldest hymns describe the rapture of the soul that has been assured of its pardon:

O how shall I the goodness tell,
Father, which thou to me hast showed?
That I, a child of wrath and hell,
I should be called a child of God!
Should know, should feel my sins forgiven,
Blest with this antepast of heaven!

Hymnals:
UM (1989),
no. 342

"antepast"
= "fore-
taste"

'Tis Love! 'tis Love! Thou diedst for me,
I hear thy whisper in my heart.
The morning breaks, the shadows flee,
pure, Universal Love thou art.

Hymnals:
AMEZ
(1957), no.
324; UM
(1989), no.
386

We should perhaps think of the experience of assurance as related to the earlier experiences of awakening and repentance: in a culture that could become emotionally distraught at the thought of one's own sinfulness, assurance came as the corresponding sense of relief from the terror of sin and judgment. For persons formed in a different cultural context, the experience of justification may take different forms. For example, "assurance" might appear as a sense of "direction" in one's life following the typical directionlessness of contemporary life. In this regard it may be important also to realize that some particular views of how justification and assurance must occur are culturally conditioned. The use of a "sinner's prayer" or the "altar call" at the end of an evangelistic service (to take two common examples) developed in the early 1800s in North

American revivals and need not be seen as normative for Christians of all times and places. Christians have experienced faith (and assurance) in a variety of ways.

The Path of Sancti- fication

"New Birth" or Regenera- tion

UM Con- fession 9

The Christian believer not only dies to sin in justification but also is "born again" to a new life in Christ. This *new birth* or *regeneration* marks the beginning of the quest for Christian holiness, or sanctification. As we shall see in the next chapter, Wesley himself believed that new birth (as well as justification) occurs at baptism, at least in the case of infants (see chapter 5). But for those capable of mature faith, it occurs simultaneously with justification in the moment a person comes to believe in Christ. Moreover, he believed that most people, even those baptized as infants, had "sinned away" the grace they had once known and so stood in need of renewal.

UM Con- fession 11; AME cat- echism, qqu. 9-14, 31-32

Trans- formed Will and Affections

New birth is the beginning of the new life in Christ, a life of growth in holiness. The term Methodists have historically favored to describe growth in holiness is *sanctification* (from *sanctus,* "holy"). But sanctification does not mean a joyless pursuit of good works or grudging restraint from things we would really like to do but know we should not. Rather, on the Wesleyan understanding, sanctification denotes in the first place the transformation of our wills and affections. We as human beings come to love and desire that which God loves, so that the pursuit of sanctification is the pursuit of ultimate joy, and we do what is right and avoid what is evil because that is what our transformed wills truly desire. In Charles Wesley's words,

I want a principle within of watchful, godly fear,
a sensibility of sin, a pain to feel it near.

Methodists often call upon believers to *renew* their commitment to Christ or to *rededicate* themselves to Christ.

An important aspect of the pursuit of sanctification is the careful following of God's *moral law*. Wesley and the Methodist doctrinal statements acknowledge, in harmony with the Reformed tradition, that the "ceremonial law" of the Hebrew Bible had passed out of use for Christians. But they insisted that the moral law remained as a guide to Christians. The content of the moral law includes preeminently the Ten Commandments. Methodist observance of the Lord's Day (see chapter 7) was grounded in their sense that the observance of Sunday as a day of rest fulfilled the commandment to sanctify the sabbath.

John Wesley's observation of persons' spiritual lives led him to identify and categorize a range of spiritual problems or illnesses that the believer might face in the quest of sanctification: temptation, fear, false security, boasting of spiritual accomplishments, forms of religious depression. Many of his sermons address these issues under titles that are sometimes simply descriptive but frequently employ biblical images: "Wandering Thoughts," "Heaviness through Manifold Temptations," and "The Wilderness State," for example. The latter title (the image is that of Israel in the wilderness, grumbling against God) indicates what Wesley considered to be the ultimate spiritual problem: loss of faith in Christ,

Marginal notes:

Hymnals: UM (1989), no. 410; "want" = "lack" or "need"

Moral Law

Articles 6; AME Catechism, qqu. 19-20

Identifying Spiritual Problems

J. Wesley, sermons on "Wandering Thoughts," "Heaviness through Manifold Temptations," "The Wilderness State" which would imply loss of one's justification. Sometimes Methodists have spoken informally of the loss of faith and justification as *falling from grace* (cf. Hebrews 6:4-6). In affirming the possibility of losing faith and justification, Methodists reject the doctrine of "eternal security" taught in some churches (especially Reformed churches, and many Baptist churches).

Sanctification and Christian Community

In the Wesleyan pattern, the quest for sanctification is not a lonely quest. It is a quest undertaken in company, with the whole system of Methodist class meetings, societies, bands, and other groupings as means to assist the seeker and the believer. It is a quest undertaken with the aid

Sanctification and the "Means of Grace"

of the "means of grace" such as prayerful Bible study, prayer, and the Lord's Supper (see the next chapter), all graciously provided by God and by means of which seekers and believers alike may have constant access to divine grace.

Social Sanctification

In the Wesleyan pattern, moreover, sanctification is not limited to the holiness of individual persons. It is a process in which believers seek the sanctification of the world around them. John Wesley himself encouraged the Methodists to take part in a wide range of movements for the betterment of social conditions. For instance, in one of his last letters Wesley passionately encouraged William Wilberforce's efforts to end human slavery in British territories. After Wesley's time Methodists involved themselves in efforts to improve conditions for laborers, women and children, to end gambling, to control consumption of alcohol, to combat racism, and to act "In Defense of Creation" (the title of a declaration on nuclear proliferation by UM bishops). Thus, the Methodist "way of salvation" leads not only inward but also outward. It leads to a comprehensive moral vision (see chapter 7) in which the transformation of the whole world is sought. But Methodists seek even this transformation, the transformation of the broader world, not by our own effort or goodness but (as ever) by divine grace.

Methodist piety describes the goal of sanctification as *entire sanctification* or *Christian perfection*. If the notion of perfection is offensive, it is also biblical: Jesus taught us to "Be perfect, therefore, as your heavenly Father is perfect" (Matthew 5:48). And to what perfection can human beings aspire? Methodists have always answered this by repeating the Great Commandment: "You shall love the Lord your God with all your heart, and with all your soul, and with all your mind" (Matthew 22:37; cf. Mark 12:30, Luke 10:27). Along with this, Methodists insist that Christian perfection also means the fulfillment of the second commandment: love of our neighbor. Thus, Christian perfection or entire sanctification denotes primarily the perfection of our love for God and for our neighbor.

The Goal of Sanctification: Entire Sanctification or Christian Perfection

UM Confession 11; AME Catechism, qqu. 80-95

John Wesley and Methodist teachers clarified that there are many ways in which human beings cannot be perfect: in this life we are never free from infirmities, temptations, mistakes, or ignorance. But when asked to justify their claim that we should look forward to (in eighteenth-century parlance, "expect") Christian perfection in this life, they responded with two related claims. (1) It is the *intention* of God that we should love God completely (again, the Great Commandment).

Wesley, sermon on "Christian Perfection" I:1-9

Wesley, sermon on "The Scripture Way of Salvation" III: 14-15

(2) It is within the *power* of God to bring about that which God intends. To deny the doctrine of Christian perfection, as they understood it, meant to deny one or the other of these central Christian claims. Although John Wesley doubted many claims to having been entirely sanctified (especially when individuals boasted about it), he believed that there were saints through the ages and in his own time who had been sanctified entirely by divine grace. Thus he asked his assistants (and Methodist churches still ask candidates for ordination): "Do you expect to be [i.e., look forward to being] made perfect in love in this life?"

The "Way of Salvation" as a Distinctively Methodist Way of Life

From the first stirrings of grace in the human soul through the consummation of God's work in entire sanctification, the Wesleyan understanding of the "way of salvation" offers a comprehensive vision of the Christian life. It is this vision that our mothers and fathers in the faith have sung and preached and taught and lived. One aspect of the beauty of this vision lies in its *balance:* the Wesleyan vision attempts to balance justification and sanctification, divine grace and human responsibility, faith and good works, personal and social holiness. Another aspect of its beauty lies in its *depth:* the Wesleyan vision is not a simple pattern, there is a depth of experience reflected in John Wesley's sermons and a depth of poetic beauty expressed in Charles Wesley's hymns. This depth is amplified in the historic experience of Methodist people who sought to live out a life of fidelity to the Savior. The understanding of the "way of salvation," then, is one of Methodism's spiritual treasures: a distinct vision of the Christian life that seeks comprehensive transformation by God's grace. In our time, we should not only be inspired by the pattern of the "way of salvation" as it appeared in the eighteenth century. We should be asking how people experience divine grace today.

Resources and References: For some specific comparisons to the Wesleyan "Way of Salvation" among Holiness and Pentecostal churches, cf. Campbell, *Christian Confessions*, pp. 235-39. A helpful guide to the "way of salvation" written for Christian leaders is given by Kenneth Cain Kinghorn, *The Gospel of Grace: The Way of Salvation in the Wesleyan Tradition* (Nashville: Abingdon Press, 1992). Some more critical studies of the Wesleyan way of salvation include the following: Albert C. Outler, *Theology in the Wesleyan Spirit* (Nashville: Discipleship Resources, 1975); Randy L. Maddox, *Responsible Grace: John Wesley's Practical Theology* (Nashville: Kingswood Books, 1994); and Kenneth J. Collins, *The Scripture Way of Salvation: The Heart of John Wesley's Theology* (Nashville: Abingdon Press, 1997).

CHAPTER 5

Doctrines About Church, Ministry, and Sacraments

Teachings About Church, Ministry, and Sacraments

The Methodist movement did not set out to be a church and only ended up becoming separate churches through a series of unfortunate circumstances. As Methodists became more conscious of their identity as members of Methodist churches or denominations, it became necessary to clarify their understandings of the church, its ministries, and its most significant acts (including its sacraments). In most cases, Methodists inherited these teachings from their roots in the Church of England and in the broader Christian tradition, although there are some distinctive Methodist notes or adjuncts to these doctrines.

Church

The thirteenth Article of Religion defines the "church" (in this case, meaning the universal Christian church) as involving three necessary elements: *faith* ("a congregation of faithful" people), *preaching* ("in which the pure Word of God is preached"), and *sacraments* ("and the Sacraments duly administered"). This definition is common to the Protestant Reformation; in fact, it echoes very closely the wording of the Anglican

Articles 13; cf. UM Confession 5

Article and the Lutheran Augsburg Confession before it.

But beyond these three necessary elements of the church there is a fourth element that gives a distinctively Methodist nuance to the understanding of church. It is characteristic of the distinctly Methodist doctrinal statements (e.g., the preface to the General Rules) to insist on a particular form of *discipline* or accountability as a distinct element of Christian fellowship. In a sense, this is held in common with the Reformed tradition (Presbyterians and Congregationalists), which had also insisted on church discipline in addition to faith, preaching, and sacraments. But whereas the Reformed tradition practiced this discipline at the level of local congregations (where the pastor and elders, for example, controlled access to communion), the Methodists practiced this discipline and accountability at the level of smaller groups of believers. In early Methodist societies, class leaders issued tickets to admit men and women to the Love Feast (see below). Disciplined accountability in small groups has been a distinctly Methodist nuance of the understanding of "church," and the original stress of the Methodist *Discipline* was on this distinct form of accountable discipleship (see chapter 7). With this stress on accountability within voluntary societies, the Methodist movement within the Church of England offered an alternative account of the meaning of Christian fellowship.

Need for Discipline and Accountability

The UM Confession of Faith follows the Nicene Creed in describing the church as "one holy catholic and apostolic." These four adjectives are historically called the "notes" of the

Notes of the Church

Nicene Creed; UM Confession 5

church and they describe the ideal church, the model which is only partially recognized as the church exists in the world and the goal towards which the Christian community is destined by God. The church will be *one* in Christ, and we work and pray for its unity here. The church is *holy* insofar as it is called apart from the world, but its holiness is only partial in the present time. The church is *catholic* because it is intended to be universal (for all people) and to embrace the fullness of Christian teaching, but its catholicity will not be fully realized until it truly is an inclusive and faithful community. The church is *apostolic* insofar as it stands in continuity with the apostolic witness, but the church always stands in need of reformation to call it back to its apostolic witness.

One (Unity)

Holy (Holiness)

Catholic (Catholicity)

Apostolic (Apostolicity)

The Church's Ministry

Within the fellowship of the church there are many "varieties of gifts" (1 Corinthians 12:4) and many functions and offices. The AME declaration on "Apostolic Succession" states that "each and every member [of the church] is a king and priest under God." Similarly, the United Methodist *Discipline* states that all baptized Christians are "ministers," in that they all have gifts for service and ministry in the church. Some within the body of believers are *ordained* for particular ministries. Since the early 100s A.D. Christians have typically recognized three orders of ministry: deacons, priests (or "presbyters" or "elders"), and bishops. Methodists inherited this threefold pattern of ordained ministry from the Church of England with two nuances: Methodists preferred to call the second order "elders" rather than "priests," and they regarded

Ordained Ministry

bishops as a higher degree of elders rather than a third order of ministry.[†] This understanding of *episcopacy* (the office of bishop) has affected Methodist relationships with other churches. In more recent ecumenical discussions, such as the WCC Faith and Order study of *Baptism, Eucharist and Ministry* (1982) or the *COCU Consensus,* Methodists have signaled their willingness to consider the historic threefold ordering of ordained ministry for the sake of ecumenical unity (see below for more on the role of bishops).

Historically, Methodist *deacons* were persons preparing for ordained ministry as elders, and the office of deacon was simply a probationary and transitional office. This is still the case in the AME, AMEZ, and CME churches. The UM Church has reshaped the diaconate (the office of deacon) in recent years to allow for *permanent* (not transitional) deacons, persons committed to ministries of love, justice, and service. The UM Church is at one with Catholics, Anglicans, and others who have moved in recent years to restore the integrity of the office of permanent deacon.

Deacons

"Transitional" Deacons

"Permanent" Deacons

In common speech Methodist *elders* are more often referred to as "ordained ministers" or "preachers" (but see below on lay preachers). Elders are ordained to preach and celebrate the sacraments. The UM Church states that elders are ordained to "word, sacrament, and order," where "order" refers both to the pastor's role in accountable discipleship (see above) and to the role typically exercised by bishops (see below) in ordaining and overseeing the church's ministries. One historic characteristic of the Methodist

Elders

Itinerant Ministry

office of elders is their *itinerant* ministry. This originally meant that the elders traveled about from place to place, preaching in a different location from day to day as they followed large circuits. In American episcopal Methodist churches the circuits have been reduced to the point that congregations expect the same pastor from week to week. Itinerancy still refers to the distinctly Methodist manner of appointing elders, where bishops in consultation with churches and "Presiding Elders" (AME, AMEZ, CME) or "District Superintendents" (UM) assign elders to their pastoral charges. The Methodist itinerancy gave Methodists as a whole an advantage in evangelization through the 1800s, by allowing a particular flexibility in following the expanding American frontier.

Presiding Elders or District Superintendents

Bishops

The commanding generals of this Methodist rapid deployment force were the *bishops*. The term "episcopal" in the name of the AME, AMEZ, and CME churches (and the older ME and MES churches) indicates the prominence of bishops in the governance of these churches. As indicated above, Methodists historically viewed bishops as elders set apart for the particular and personal ministry of superintending the church (not as a separate order of ministry). Like the bishops of other Christian communions (Orthodox, Catholic, and Anglican), Methodist bishops are elected for life and represent the church in performing ordinations. Unlike these other Christian communions, however, Methodists do not insist on an unbroken succession of bishops from the ancient church. The AME Church statement on "Apostolic Succession" makes it clear

No Necessity of "Apostolic Succession"; AME Statement on "Apostolic Succession"

that Methodist ministerial orders do not rely on a literal succession of bishops from the apostles. We should note that at least one constituent member of the UM Church, the Methodist Protestant Church, had rejected the idea of episcopacy (the office of bishop) altogether, and the EUB Church had "term" bishops (bishops elected to serve a specified term, not acknowledged as a bishop for life). Finally, it is appropriate to note that Methodist churches, through the *COCU Consensus,* have signaled their willingness to consider and possibly embrace more historic forms of episcopacy in which apostolic succession is maintained, even though this move would not imply belief that apostolic succession is necessary to the existence of the church.

Other Ministerial Offices

Beyond the deacons, elders, and bishops that answer to the three orders of historic churches, Methodists have historically employed a number of different ministerial offices. From very early on, laypersons preached among the Methodists.

Lay Preachers

John Wesley tried to clarify that they were "extraordinary" ministers who were not usurping the "ordinary" ministries of (Anglican) priests.

Lay or Local Preachers

Almost all Methodist churches have employed some form of *lay preaching* ministry, although the authority given to lay preachers (or "local preachers") to celebrate the sacraments has varied from time to time. Lay or local preachers are trained by the church, and thousands of smaller Methodist churches have been kept alive through the efforts of lay preachers.

Deaconesses

In the nineteenth century, Methodist churches trained and consecrated women as *deaconesses* for particular service-oriented ministries. The AME Church continues to do so. Their ministries form one of the historic precedents for UM renewal of the office of permanent deacon in recent decades. Beyond these offices, Methodist churches have employed laypersons in numerous offices, such as those of stewards, class leaders, and persons who serve on the church's boards and committees. The UMC continues the tradition of the older Methodist Protestant Church in insisting on equal lay and clergy representation on all connectional conferences.

Means of Grace

An important part of Methodist teaching about the church is our belief that grace is to be found through regular channels appointed by God. John Wesley defended what he called the *means of grace,* which he defined as "outward signs, words, or actions, ordained of God, and appointed for this end, to be the ordinary channels whereby he might convey to men, preventing, justifying, or sanctifying grace." In his sermon "The Means of Grace," written in contention with a particular group of London Moravians, Wesley named prayer, "searching the Scriptures," and the Lord's Supper. In the "General Rules" our churches affirm that we are to seek Christ by "attending upon all the ordinances of God," which are specified as follows: public worship, preaching, the Lord's Supper, private and family prayer, Scripture study, and fasting. John Wesley acknowledged that the "means of grace" were not limited to those explicitly named in Scripture: he recognized even in the experience of the Methodist people that some activities, such as the regular visiting of the societies by the preachers, were found in practical

J. Wesley, Sermon on "The Means of Grace" II:1

"General Rules" Part III

experience to be means of grace. In subsequent Methodist experience, camp meetings and revivals were found, similarly, to be means of divine grace. Thus the CME *Discipline* has a separate chapter on the "Means of Grace," which includes discussion of the Lord's Supper and the Love Feast (see below).

Among the means of grace, Wesley's sermons and the "General Rules" always name the Lord's Supper. Baptism is not named among them, because the lists of means of grace or "ordinances of God" include the means to be used regularly or repeatedly by Christians. Like other Protestant churches, the Methodist churches acknowledge baptism and the Lord's Supper as *sacraments,* which our sixteenth Article of Religion defines as "certain signs of grace, and God's good will toward us, by the which he doth work invisibly in us." This article implies that sacraments (a) are ordained by Christ with a command that we should continue them; (b) have an outward and "visible" sign (water, or the elements of wine and bread); and (c) somehow convey divine grace to those who receive them with faith. Methodist elders have authority to celebrate the sacraments; the various Methodist denominations have differed from time to time over the issue of whether lay or local preachers and deacons could celebrate the sacraments (see above).

With almost all Christian communities, Methodists practice *baptism* following Christ's command (Matthew 28:19) as the sacrament of Christian initiation, the means by which persons are brought into the fellowship of the church. Methodists have not found it easy to come to a consensus about the relationship between bap-

Margin notes:

Sacraments

Articles 16; UM Confession 6

Baptism

tism and salvation. Consider the following range of views on this issue:

Option 1: Baptism as Outward Sign of Christian Identification

1. Some churches have insisted that baptism is only an outward sign of membership, and so has no direct relationship to our salvation (the belief favored by churches that practice believers' baptism, and by many Protestant liberals).

Option 2: Baptism as Linked to Justification and Regeneration

2. Churches of the Reformed tradition insisted that baptism is connected or linked to our justification and regeneration (new birth), but not "automatically": the moment when water was applied might be different from the moment when a person was justified and born again.

Option 3: Baptism as the Means of Justification and Regeneration

3. Other Christian traditions, including those of Eastern Orthodox, Roman Catholic, Lutheran churches, and Wesley's own Anglican Church have insisted that baptism is itself the means of justification and regeneration, that is, that those who have been baptized have been justified and born again.

J. Wesley, Sermon on "The New Birth" IV:1-2

Articles 17

John Wesley affirmed the third position with respect to the baptism of infants. However, he warned that mature persons cannot "rely on" baptism, since it is possible to deny the faith into which one was baptized. Moreover, our Article of Religion on baptism (17) deletes a significant passage from the Anglican Article (on which it is based) which states that

> as by an instrument, they that receive Baptism rightly are grafted into the Church; the prom-

ises of forgiveness of sin, and our adoption to be the sons of God by the Holy Ghost, are visibly signed and sealed; Faith is confirmed, and Grace increased by virtue of prayer unto God.

[Omitted from Methodist Article]

Because this passage contains the strongest language about baptism as an "instrument," its omission inclines the Methodist understanding of baptism toward the second historic position given above. Similarly, the UM Confession of Faith describes baptism as a "symbol of repentance and inner cleansing from sin." In fact, a recent UMC document on baptism (1996) affirms a position very similar to that of the historic Reformed churches, namely, that the moment of application of the water in baptism cannot be identified precisely as the moment when a person is born again. We should emphasize at this point that despite disagreements over the relationship between baptism and salvation, there is wide agreement that baptism is the means appointed by Christ by which persons are ingrafted into the fellowship of the church.

UM Confession 6

UM Baptismal Study, affirmed in 1996

Methodist churches agree in practicing *infant baptism* (this is affirmed explicitly in the seventeenth Article), and historically have expended considerable energy defending the practice of infant baptism in response to churches that practice believers' baptism only. The practice of infant baptism is grounded in the household baptisms recorded in the New Testament (Acts 16:15, 16:33), Jesus' invitation to the children (Matthew 19:13-15, Mark 10:13-16, Luke 18:15-17), and in the consideration that infants as well as others need the fellowship of the church. We

Infant Baptism

Articles 17; UM Confession 6

might note, though, that in affirming the WCC study of *Baptism, Eucharist and Ministry* (1982) and in rearranging hymnals to place the order for adult baptism first, Methodist churches reflect a growing ecumenical trend to see adult baptism as the normative expression of baptism in the church. This does not contradict the continued practice of infant baptism, but it suggests that infant baptism should be seen as a special or exceptional possibility open to children of mature believers.

Modes of Baptism: Sprinkling, Pouring, Immersion

Methodist churches allow the practice of baptism by *sprinkling, pouring,* or *immersion.* The fact that very few Methodist church buildings have large baptisteries means that immersion is seldom a practical choice. Again, however, growing ecumenical consensus has led Methodists with other Christians to consider more seriously the option of baptism by immersion, the church's most ancient mode of baptism.

The Lord's Supper

The second sacrament affirmed by Methodists along with the historic Christian community is the sacrament of *the Lord's Supper* (we will sometimes call it "Holy Communion," and in ecumenical contexts, the "Eucharist"). In this act we celebrate our fellowship or communion with Christ and with each other, and we recognize the new grace that Christ offers us. As we considered baptism above in relationship to three historic viewpoints, so we may consider the Lord's Supper in relation to the following four historic understandings:

Option 1: Memorialism or Zwinglianism

1. Some churches maintain that the Lord's Supper is merely a memorial or reminder of Christ's sacrifice and a sign of Christian fel-

lowship. Many Evangelical churches and a minority in the Reformed churches have maintained this "Zwinglian" understanding of the Supper.

2. Historic Reformed churches maintain that although Christ's body ascended to heaven, the Supper of the Lord, when received with true faith, conveys a unique spiritual power. Because the Latin term for this spiritual power is *virtus,* this perspective is sometimes described as "virtualism." — Option 2: Virtualism

3. Lutheran churches maintain that Christ's true, human body is present with the elements of bread and wine in the celebration of the supper. This perspective is often described as belief in the "corporeal" (bodily) presence of Christ. — Option 3: Corporeal Presence

4. Historic Roman Catholic teaching maintains not only that Christ's human body is present, but that the essence of bread and wine are changed, with only their physical, visible reality persisting. This perspective is historically described as "transubstantiation." — Option 4: Transubstantiation

The eighteenth Article of Religion explicitly rules out the medieval formulation of the latter doctrine (transubstantiation), and the introduction to this Article as well as the Wesleys' own eucharistic devotion would seem to call the first option into question. Certainly Charles Wesley's hymns evoke faith in more than a merely symbolic presence of Christ: "O taste the goodness of our God,/and eat his flesh and drink his blood." — Articles 18 — Hymnals: UM (1989), no. 616

Sometimes Charles Wesley utilized the precise language of virtualism: "Who explains the wondrous way, how through these [elements] the virtue came?/ These the virtue did convey, yet still remain the same." The Article (18) can be read as allowing for either virtualism or belief in corporeal presence. Our Anglican sisters and brothers often avoid the need for the distinction by referring to the "real presence" of Christ in the sacrament, since "real presence" can denote either of these views, although this term has not been used in historic Methodist doctrinal sources. Without the need for a precise definition of this, we should nevertheless approach Holy Communion in such a way that we expect to meet Christ in the sacrament.

Hymnals: UM (1989), no. 627

"Real Presence"

It is the custom of Methodist churches to practice *open communion,* that is, our communion is open to all Christians. This longstanding custom is not grounded in doctrinal sources, and in fact the early Methodist societies practiced a very strict communion, access to which was sometimes controlled by class tickets in the same manner as the Love Feast (see below). Methodists may appeal to John Wesley's claim that communion could be a "converting ordinance"[†] to justify the liberality of our invitation to partake of the Lord's Supper. While this might justify the communion of baptized unbelievers (Wesley was convinced that there were plenty of them), it does not address the issue of communion across denominational lines, which is the main intent of our openness in the invitation to receive the elements. The issue of open communion is ecumenically sensitive, not only because

Open Communion

Methodists react negatively to the practice of strict or "close" communion in other churches, but also because other churches may regard Methodist liberality as promiscuity, especially when individuals extend the invitation to non-baptized or non-Christian persons.

John and Charles Wesley advocated *frequent communion*. They maintained that refusal to commune, when the opportunity was available, was essentially rejecting Christ. John Wesley stated in 1784 that he expected every Methodist elder to celebrate the Lord's Supper every Sunday.[†] The practice of preaching in large circuits, however, meant that elders were not present every Sunday to every Methodist society (or church), and so congregations early on became accustomed to infrequent communion. Efforts for Wesleyan renewal in recent decades, as well as ecumenical contact, have encouraged Methodists to recover the grace of frequent communion. Here the challenging words of Charles Wesley apply: "Do not begin to make excuse; ah! do not you his grace refuse; /your worldly cares and pleasures leave, and take what Jesus hath to give."

Frequent Communion

Hymnals: UM (1989), no. 616

We have mentioned above that John Wesley considered sacraments to be a part of the broader category of "means of grace." Methodists have recognized other means as well. The *Love Feast* was a primitive Christian institution revived by Moravians in John Wesley's time and taken up by the early Methodist societies. The Love Feast was celebrated quarterly by Methodist societies, and admission to it was controlled by issuing class tickets indicating faithful participation in

Other Means of Grace

Love Feast
Watch-night

the class and keeping the General Rules. Another distinctly Methodist institution (also with early Christian precedents) was the *watchnight,* when Methodists would spend whole nights in prayer together, following the institution of "vigils" in the early church. Later Methodists would find camp meetings and revivals to be means of divine grace.

The Church, the Means of Grace, and the Christian Life

Compared to the older, more liturgical churches, Methodists often appear to be freewheeling, informal, and evangelical in their styles of worship and church life. Compared to evangelical churches, on the other hand, Methodists appear to be somewhat more formal, more liturgical, and more "churchly." One of the gifts of the Methodist movement is to offer a "churchly" or sacramental vision of evangelical faith. Our teachings on the nature of the church, its ministries, and its means of grace including its sacraments, describe the "churchly" side of Methodist spirituality. But these are related directly to the quest for grace described in the previous chapter: Wesley's own definition of "means of grace" states that what they convey is prevenient, justifying, and sanctifying grace (see chapter 4).

Resources and References: For general comparative materials on doctrines about the church and sacraments, cf. Campbell, *Christian Confessions,* pp. 54-61 (Eastern Orthodoxy), 97-112 (Roman Catholicism), 163-83 (Reformation and Union churches), and 240-56 (Evangelical and Free churches). The belief that bishops were a higher degree of elders rather than a third order of ministry was claimed in the Latitudinarian sources Wesley read in the 1750s and to whom he referred in justifying his ordinations of 1784 (Edward Still-ingfleet and Peter King). The same sources are cited by Bishops Asbury and Coke in their published notes to the earliest ME *Discipline, The Doctrines and Disciplines of the Methodist Episcopal Church in America, with Explanatory Notes* (Philadelphia: Henry Tuckniss, 1798), pp. 45-46. John Wesley's reference to the Lord's Supper as a "converting ordinance" comes in a summary of a sermon reported in his *Journal* (27 June 1740). John Wesley's exhortation to the elders to celebrate the Lord's Supper every Sunday is found in the prefatory letter to the *Sunday Service of the Methodists in North America* (¶4, p. ii).

CHAPTER 6

DOCTRINES ABOUT JUDGMENT, ETERNAL LIFE, AND THE REIGN OF GOD

Teachings About Judgment, Eternal Life, and the Reign of God

Because we live by our visions, our beliefs about the future affect our daily lives. This is as true of groups of people as it is for individuals: a marriage, for example, may withstand any number of problems so long as a common vision or goal is shared. In describing teachings about judgment, eternal life, and the reign of God, we are really describing our tradition's understanding of a common vision for God's future. Though dealing with those matters, this is a shorter chapter because Christian doctrine has not focused extensively on these issues, and they are dealt with rather briefly in Methodist doctrinal sources.

Judgment

Articles 3; cf. UM Confession 12

Apostles' Creed and Nicene Creed

The third Article of Religion affirms that Christ "ascended into heaven, and there sitteth until he return to judge all men at the last day." This statement is consistent with the Apostles' Creed ("from thence he shall come to judge the quick and the dead") and the Nicene Creed ("He will come again in glory to judge the living and the dead"). In the end, Christ will be our judge. Wesley's *Sermons* maintain that at the final judgment every one of our thoughts, words, and deeds will be known and judged. Our justification on "the last day" will again be by faith in Christ (see chapters 3 and 4), but our works will not escape God's examination. Charles Wesley's hymn "Lo, He Comes with Clouds Descending" paints a graphic portrait of this judgment: "Every eye shall now behold him, robed in dreadful majesty. . . ."

Hymnals: AME (1984), no. 99; UM (1989), no. 718

Historic Methodist doctrine affirms, with the broader Christian tradition, that those who have been saved by Christ will share the joy of eternal fellowship with Christ and the saints. The Apostles' Creed concludes by affirming our belief in "the life everlasting"; similarly, the Nicene Creed concludes with an affirmation of "the life of the world to come." *Heaven* simply means eternal joy in Christ, in John Wesley's terms, "eternal happiness." The judgment reserved for those who reject Christ *(hell)* is "endless condemnation" (UM Confession), to be divorced finally from this eternal joy in Christ and fellowship with the saints. The church and its members never dare to make this judgment. In the end, we believe that "the judge of all the earth [will] do what is just" (Genesis 18:25), that is, the final judgment will reflect God's perfect justice.

Eternal Life in Christ

Apostles' Creed and Nicene Creed; UM Confession 12

J. Wesley, Sermon on "The Scripture Way of Salvation," I:1

The Methodist Articles of Religion, following the teachings of the Reformation, rejected the medieval Catholic idea of *purgatory* as a place where the souls of those who have died in Christ could be aided or helped by the prayers of the living. John Wesley himself believed in an intermediate state between death and the final judg-

Articles 14

ment, where those who rejected Christ would be aware of their coming doom (not yet pronounced), and believers would share in the "bosom of Abraham" or "paradise," even continuing to grow in holiness there. This belief, however, is not formally affirmed in Methodist doctrinal standards, which reject the idea of purgatory but beyond that maintain silence on what lies between death and the last judgment.

The Kingdom or Reign of God

Nicene Creed

The last thing the Nicene Creed says about Christ is that "his kingdom will have no end." This refers to the biblical theme of the coming reign or kingdom of God, a message consistently on the lips of Jesus as Matthew, Mark, and Luke depict him. The "kingdom of God" is more than a personal vision of God's future: it implies a future in which God's reign or rule affects the whole world. It is a vision of the transformation of the earth until God's justice, mercy, and love prevail throughout the whole. Recent studies have shown that as John Wesley grew older his belief in the scope of salvation grew. His belief that the "new creation" would involve the redemption and healing of every aspect of the universe, only hinted at earlier in his life, became much more explicit. Although this vision for the redemption of the whole of creation is not as explicit in Methodist doctrinal sources as it is in John Wesley's later writings, it can provide a powerful basis for a renewed Wesleyan social and ecological vision today.

J. Wesley, sermon on "The New Creation"

Living by the Christian Hope

We are called to live in hope, a hope (again!) "built on nothing less than Jesus' blood and righteousness" (Edward Mote). God's grace will change us, will change our Christian community, and in the end will transform the entirety of creation. At last it will be said that "The kingdom of the world has become the kingdom of our Lord and of his Messiah, and he will reign forever and ever" (Revelation 11:15).

Resources and References: For some comparative materials on life beyond death, cf. Campbell, *Christian Confessions,* pp. 53-54 (Eastern Orthodoxy), 96-97 (Roman Catholicism), 162 (Reformation and Union churches), and 239-40 (Evangelical and Free churches). On the idea of the "new creation" in Wesley's later thought and its relevance for contemporary Wesleyan life, see Theodore M. Runyon, *The New Creation: John Wesley's Theology Today* (Nashville: Abingdon Press, 1998). John Wesley's belief in an intermediate state between death and the final judgment is expressed in his sermons on "The Good Steward" II:1-2 and "The Important Question" II:4.

Hymnals: AME (1984), no. 364; AMEZ (1957), no. 251; CME (1987), no. 223; UM (1989), no. 368

CHAPTER 7

METHODIST DOCTRINE AND METHODIST ETHOS

Doctrine, Morality, and Ethos   A book on Christian doctrine would not necessarily discuss matters of Christian ethics and morality, but the truth is that many of the Methodist doctrinal standards (especially the General Rules and the Social Creed) are concerned with Christian morality. As we have seen in the introduction, Methodist doctrine has consistently included moral as well as theological affirmations, and Methodist membership was based largely on ethical, not doctrinal, tests. Many of the ethical issues addressed in older Methodist doctrinal statements seem antiquated today (for example, regarding the payment of certain tariffs) or simply quaint (observance of Sunday as the Lord's Day). But it is important to include even in this concise work at least a sketch of the Methodist *ethos* (way of life) expressed in our doctrinal statements. Because of our focus on the historic ethos of Methodist churches, this chapter will not address such critical contemporary ethical issues as abortion or homosexuality, although some Methodist churches have adopted contemporary statements regarding these issues.

In describing what a truly Christian society might look like, C. S. Lewis speculated that we might find that "its economic life was very socialistic, and, in that sense 'advanced,' but that its family life and code of manners were rather old-fashioned."† The same might be said of the historic Methodist ethos, but in very particular ways. With respect to personal morality it was a rather strict or stern view of life, stressing moral responsibility, the need to engage in good works, and the need to avoid such specific evils as smoking or drinking alcoholic beverages. With respect to social morality, however, the Methodist ethos tended to be rather more progressive, involving Methodist churches in the struggles to eradicate slavery and racism in the United States, and to champion the needs of women and children in society.

Methodist Ethos: Strict Personal Morality and Progressive Social Morality

We should be clear in entering a discussion of historic Methodist morality that the Methodist ethos did not understand moral life as a dull matter of sullenly avoiding really enticing evils and grudgingly doing what someone else regarded as good. As we have seen in chapter 4, Methodists understood that in the pursuit of sanctification a person's will and affections were progressively transformed, so that by grace one came to the point where one genuinely disliked evil and genuinely desired to do good. In practice, sermons and hymns often provided motivation by which a community was empowered to avoid named evils and to do all manner of good: "Rescue the perishing, care for the dying; Jesus is merciful, Jesus will save" (Fanny Crosby). Gracious moti-

Ground of the Methodist Ethos: Transformed Affections

Hymnals: AME (1984), no. 211; CME (1987), no. 142; UM (1989), no. 591

vation (motivation that flows from divine grace) was as important for Methodist social morality as it was for personal morality. Avoiding evil and doing good were to flow from repentance, faith, and joy in Christ.

Organization of This Chapter

This chapter will attempt to describe the historic Methodist ethos expressed in our doctrinal statements under the three general headings of (1) life in the Christian community; (2) personal morality; and (3) social morality. The doctrinal sources most generally utilized are the General Rules, a few items in the Articles of Religion that relate to issues of morality, passages in John Wesley's *Sermons* that relate to issues of Christian conduct and morality, and the Methodist Social Creed. Beyond this, we shall indicate a few further areas of consistent moral consensus in Methodist communities, implied though not explicitly stated in historic doctrinal statements.

Life in the Christian Community

The three headings of the General Rules are (1) to avoid evil of all sorts; (2) to do good of all sorts; and (3) to attend upon all the "ordinances of God." Life in the Christian community is the underlying presupposition of the General Rules, which functioned as a kind of contract by which Methodists held each other accountable from week to week for their moral conduct. The General Rules hold Methodists specifically accountable for the following items related to life in the Christian community under the third category of the "ordinances of God":

General Rules, Part III; cf. UM Confession, item 13

The public worship of God

The ministry of the Word, either read or expounded

The Supper of the Lord
Family and private prayer
Searching the Scriptures
Fasting or abstinence

All of these items were understood as "means of grace" (see chapter 5). Methodists at first participated in the first three items—public worship, preaching, and the Lord's Supper—in the context of the Church of England. As Methodists developed their own circuits of itinerant preachers, the second item became increasingly their own and by the 1780s Methodists had largely developed their own services of public worship, including the celebration of the Lord's Supper. As we have seen in chapter 5, however, celebration of communion among Methodists became less frequent after the Wesleys' time. Eventually, Methodist public worship would develop more distinct services and occasions such as camp meetings, urban revivals, and Sunday evening and Wednesday evening prayer services.

Public Worship, Preaching, and the Lord's Supper

The second group of three items in this list—family or personal prayer, devotional Bible study, and regular fasting—were disciplines encouraged in distinctly Methodist (as opposed to Anglican) contexts. It might be noted that fasting, for Methodists, did not need to be harsh. John Wesley's own personal practice was to avoid food from sunrise until midafternoon on Wednesdays and Fridays, following the custom of ancient Christians. The combination of these forms of more intimate spirituality with public worship, preaching, and sacramental celebration gave Methodist life a characteristic shape formed by consistent spiritual disciplines.

Prayer, Bible Study, Fasting

The Lord's Day

General Rules, Part I; cf. UM Confession, item 14

A consistent aspect of the Methodist ethos was the observance of Sunday as "the Lord's Day," including abstention from labor on that day and serious attempts to avoid causing others to labor on Sunday. The General Rules specifically prohibit Methodists from "profaning the day of the Lord, either by doing ordinary work therein or by buying or selling."

Class Meetings and Other Small Groups

Preface to the General Rules

One further aspect of Methodist ethos within the Christian community was participation in small groups, the first being Methodist "societies" which by the mid-1740s had been subdivided into more intimate "classes." It is critically important to realize that these groups met not only for prayer and Bible study, but especially for the exercise of accountable discipleship. The preface to the General Rules explains the origins of these groups and places the ethical material of the rules in the context in which they were lived by Methodists. In becoming a Methodist, one agreed to be held accountable to the General Rules, and part of the weekly discipline of Methodist classes was to inquire as to whether each member had kept the rules that week. The older structure of Methodist classes had begun to decline by the middle of the 1800s, although they persist in many of the African American Methodist churches. From the late 1800s, adult Sunday school classes and newer weekday groups for Methodist women, men, and youth took up some of the ethos of the older classes. The older ethos of accountable discipleship is currently undergoing renewal in covenant discipleship, which calls believers to organize small groups to hold each other accountable weekly to covenants developed from contemporary Christian concerns.

A second broad area in which we may describe the historic Methodist ethos has to do with teachings about *personal morality*. Methodists were expected to be above reproach in their personal conduct, and the period of probationary membership (still in effect for AME, AMEZ, and CME churches) tests an individual's personal integrity. A candidate for Methodist membership was expected to be not only *honest* but also *open*. This is why many Methodists opposed membership in "secret societies" (meaning Masonic and similar organizations). Methodist membership implied openness and vulnerability to members of one's church, especially members of one's class. Methodist conduct, above all, was to be guided by the Golden Rule.

Personal Morality

Both the General Rules and at least one of the Articles of Religion are concerned with issues of appropriate *speech*. The General Rules forbid "the taking of the name of God in vain," "fighting, quarreling, brawling, brother going to law with brother; returning evil for evil, or railing for railing; the using many words in buying or selling," and "uncharitable or unprofitable conversation; particularly speaking evil of magistrates or of ministers." The twenty-fifth Article of Religion allows that Christians may swear an oath before a magistrate when legally required, but maintains that "vain and rash swearing is forbidden Christian men by our Lord Jesus Christ and James his apostle." Methodists, then, were to guard their speech carefully, speaking only when it was necessary or helpful.

Morality with Respect to Speech

General Rules, Part I; J. Wesley, Sermon on "The Cure of Evil Speaking"

Articles 25

Sexual Purity

Another area of personal morality important for the historic Methodist ethos has to do with *sexual purity* or *chastity*. The doctrinal statements actually say very little about sexual morality, taking it as a given that the only appropriate venue for the expression of sexual intimacy was within a marriage recognized by both the state and the church. In general, Methodists were to avoid any occasion of lewdness or of sexually suggestive or provocative situations. This meant, for instance, avoidance of dance, which Methodists considered to be sexually provocative.

Dress

Yet another area of personal morality with which Methodists were concerned had to do with the manner in which one dressed. Thus, the General Rules forbid "what we know is not for the glory of God, as: The putting on of gold and costly apparel." Methodists emphasized simplicity of dress not only because dress might be sexually suggestive (see above), but also because they considered ornate dress to be an instance of improper stewardship, that is, an abuse of property. Thus, along with extravagance in dress the General Rules also forbid "Softness and needless self-indulgence." The AMEZ Church alters the General Rules at this point to rule out the wearing of gold "as a useless ornament."

General Rules, Part I

Stewardship of Money and Personal Possessions

The latter quotations raise the issue of the use of money and of personal possessions. Many Methodists are aware of John Wesley's sermon on "The Use of Money," in which he encouraged Methodists to "Gain all you can," "Save all you can," and "Give all you can." This was not, however, a license for unbridled greed. Rather, the explanations under each of these points (especially the first one) clarify that one must gain all that one can by honest industry and in such a manner that no harm is done to any other person. Wesley was intensely aware of "The Danger of Riches" (the title of another of his *Sermons*) and thought that surplus accumulation amounted to robbery of the poor. Thus the General Rules condemn "Laying up treasure upon earth." Consistent with this same ethic, Methodists were wary of lending and borrowing. The General Rules condemn both "the giving or taking things on usury i.e., unlawful interest" and "borrowing without a probability of paying; or taking up goods without a probability of paying for them." The Articles of Religion and the United Methodist Confession of Faith both allow that Christians may own private property, but Methodists were concerned with the appropriate and responsible use or stewardship of one's possessions.

J. Wesley, Sermon on "The Use of Money," I:1, and II:1

Articles 24; UM Confession, Article 15

Methodists were passionately concerned with the issue of *temperance* in the use of alcoholic beverages. At first, this meant quite literally temperance, that is, only weaker (non-distilled) alcoholic beverages could be consumed, and these in strict moderation. Thus, the General Rules forbid "Drunkenness: buying or selling spirituous liquors, or drinking them, unless in cases of extreme necessity." In eighteenth century use, "spirituous liquors" referred to distilled beverages (like whiskey or gin). The expression "cases of extreme necessity" has reference to medicinal uses of distilled beverages. Eventually, however, Methodist experience with the dangers of alcohol led them to recommend (in some

Alcohol: Temperance and Abstinence

General Rules, Part I

cases, to require) *total abstinence* from alcoholic beverages. Methodists involved themselves wholeheartedly in the struggle for prohibition of alcoholic beverages in the United States, believing that the proscription of alcohol would improve the whole of society. The AMEZ Church alters the General Rules at this point, prohibiting "spirituous *or intoxicating* liquors," making clear its commitment to total abstinence.

Worldly Amusements

General Rules, Part I

Finally, an account of the personal morality associated with the historic Methodist ethos would be incomplete without some mention of Methodist opposition to popular or "worldly" amusements. The General Rules forbid "the taking such diversions as cannot be used in the name of the Lord Jesus" and "the singing those songs, or reading those books, which do not tend to the knowledge or love of God." The AMEZ Church's version of the General Rules prohibits "dancing, card-playing, lottery, policy and other games of chance, going to circuses and theatres." Methodists have historically *opposed gambling*

Opposition to Gambling

(in some cases all "games of chance") not only because of their desire to avoid worldly amusements, but also on grounds of responsible stewardship and the disastrous effects gambling could have on one's life and on the character of one's community.

Social Morality

We now turn to consider a third area of historic Methodist ethos, namely, Methodist *social morality*. In this area, Methodists have historically taken rather progressive stands for the reform of society—in our view, the sanctification of society.

A central concern of Methodist social morality

has been the enterprise of *social outreach*. For **Outreach** the historic Methodist ethos, this did not mean simply charitable giving (see below), but concrete, face-to-face involvement with the poor, the sick, the dying, the exploited, and the suffering. The General Rules held Methodists responsible for (among other things) "giving food to the hungry . . . clothing the naked . . . visiting or helping them that are sick or in prison." The mission statement of the AME Church captures the spirit of this stress on outreach eloquently, and at the very beginning of the *Discipline:*

> The Mission of the African Methodist Episcopal Church is to minister to the spiritual, intellectual, physical and emotional, and environmental needs of all people by spreading Christ's liberating gospel through word and deed. At every level of the Connection and in every local church, the African Methodist Episcopal Church shall engage in carrying out the spirit of the original Free African Society, out of which the A.M.E. Church evolved: that is, to seek out and save the lost, and serve the needy through a continuing program of (1) preaching the gospel, (2) feeding the hungry, (3) clothing the naked, (4) housing the homeless, (5) cheering the fallen, (6) providing jobs for the jobless, (7) administering to the need of those in prisons, hospitals, nursing homes, asylums and mental institutions, senior citizens' homes, caring for the sick, the shut-in, the mentally and socially disturbed, and (8) encouraging thrift and economic advancement.[†]

Mission
Statement
of the
AME
Church

One of the enormous tragedies of Methodist history was the departure of the Salvation Army, under the leadership of Catherine and William Booth, from the Methodist New Connexion in nineteenth-century Britain. This was a tragedy because the more the Methodists identified with the middle class, the more they surrendered concrete involvement with the poor to such groups as the Salvation Army.

Charitable Giving   A second historic aspect of historic Methodist social ethos was *charitable giving*. This was linked directly to the personal ethic of responsible stewardship (above). Methodists condemned surplus accumulation of possessions (accumulation of possessions beyond the necessities of life) in the belief that any surplus belonged to God and God's poor, and the hoarding of it amounted to robbery of God and God's poor. Thus the third point of John Wesley's sermon was to "Give all you can," and the sermon makes it clear that believers are to give all they have beyond what is strictly needed. Again, the ethic of charitable giving must be seen in connection to the previous point about outreach: Methodists were not simply writing out checks to unknown organizations. Rather, they supported charitable missions with which they were themselves directly involved. In Methodist congregations, then, tithing and pledging are not simply ways to raise funds for church activities; they are an expression of spirituality.

Involvement with Systemic Social Evils   A third aspect of the Methodist social ethos was *involvement with systemic social evils* that had to be addressed in the political forum. For the Methodists of Wesley's age, the preeminent instance of systemic evil was the institution of

human *slavery,* and Wesley not only supported **Slavery**
political efforts for the abolition of slavery, he
insisted that slave-holding should preclude an
individual from being identified as a Methodist.
The General Rules from 1808 forbade "slaveholding: buying or selling slaves" (see the notes
in appendix 1).

Having said this, however, we must also say
that failure to maintain the Wesleyan witness in
regard to slavery became the single most divi-
sive issue in the first hundred years of Methodist
churches in America. Very early in its history the
ME Church compromised on the condition of
slaveholding as a bar to membership. The situa-
tion was exacerbated in the 1840s with the seces-
sion of the MES specifically over the issue of
slaveholding. Even this should not blind us to the
continuing witness of AME and AMEZ
Methodists and many in the ME Church in favor
of abolition. The ME General Conference finally restated in 1860 that slaveholding should be
grounds for removal of a person from membership, and this historic stance was belatedly reaffirmed by the successors of the MES upon their
union with the ME and MP Churches in 1939.

In addition to the issue of slavery, Methodist **Opposi-**
churches have had to face the broader issue of **tion to**
racism as a doctrinal matter. Although "racism" **Racism**
is sometimes identified simply with racial prejudice or bigotry, here we are concerned with the
sinister combination of racial bigotry with inherited power structures or systems, especially in
the churches. Although the doctrine of the
catholicity of the church (see chapter 5) should
rule out racism in all its forms, racism has been

so insinuated into modern societies and cultures that churches must deal with it in more direct and sustained ways. For Methodists, concern about racism was at first tied to the issue of slavery (see the preceding paragraphs). It appeared as a broader issue, however, at the very origins of the AME and AMEZ churches, and then most sharply in the form of segregated Methodist denominations in the period after the Civil War in the United States.

The "Historical Statement" at the beginning of every AME *Discipline* and the "Founder's Address" at the beginning of every AMEZ *Discipline* make it clear that both of these denominations originated in situations of exclusion from church structures, painful exclusion that was based entirely on racial sentiment. From the very beginning, then, these churches were concerned not only with the issue of slavery but also with the broader issues of racism as prejudice insinuated into power structures. Thus the AME "Episcopal Salutation" states "that we unequivocally stand against racism in all of its manifestations, e.g., systemic, personal, institutional, ideological, cultural and economic."

AME *Discipline* 1992, p. 3.

By contrast, the Methodist Episcopal Church, South, became a racially segregated church. When the CME church separated in 1870 from the MES Church, its original name was the "Colored Methodist Episcopal Church," and it inherited the pattern of racial segregation of the southern states, although its *Discipline* notes that "it was at no time exclusively" African American. In 1956 the denomination formally changed its name to the "Christian Methodist Episcopal"

CME *Discipline* 1994, p. 14.

Church, noting "the inconsistency of having a racial designation in the name of our church." The formal segregationist stance of the MES Church had to be dropped prior to its union with the ME and MP churches in 1939, although structurally sanctioned racial segregation persisted until 1970 in the form of the separate Central Jurisdiction. Both the CME and the UM churches now have articles asserting "The Inclusiveness of the Church" in their constitutions, and state their opposition to racism in their own versions of the Social Creed (CME) or Social Principles (UM). Members and agencies of all four Methodist churches participated in the Civil Rights movement of the 1950s and the 1960s; recent historical scholarship has brought to light the significant involvement of white, southern Methodist churchwomen in this struggle.[†]

For Methodists, opposition to racism is grounded not only in our understanding that the church is "catholic" or universal (chapter 5), but also in our Arminian theology, which insists on the universal scope of the gospel and the universal scope of our evangelistic calling (chapter 3). Charles Wesley's hymns sounded a note of radical inclusion that echoes throughout Methodist worship. It continues to echo through favorite Methodist hymns, for example, this verse of "In Christ There Is No East or West," newly revised on the basis of Galatians 3:28:

In Christ is neither Jew nor Greek,
    and neither slave nor free;
both male and female heirs are made,
    and all are kin to me.

Stanza 3 by Laurence Hull Stookey (1987); in UM *Hymnal* (1989), The United Methodist Publishing House, no. 548; cf AME (1984), no. 557; AMEZ (1957), no. 543

After the time of Wesley and the writing of our older doctrinal statements, Methodists involved themselves in other social reforming efforts. They involved themselves in efforts to ameliorate the conditions of women and children. Deaconesses (see chapter 5) stood at the forefront of Methodist social reform efforts. With the growth of American cities in the late 1800s and early 1900s, Methodists became involved in improving the conditions of laborers and persons trapped in urban poverty. Concern over these issues led the ME Church in 1908 to adopt a distinctive confessional document, the Methodist *Social Creed*.

The Methodist Social Creed Though at first primarily addressing economic and labor issues, this declaration as it evolved stated boldly the church's concern for responsible use of the earth's resources, for human rights, for just distribution of wealth, and for peace. Despite the progressive stance of this document, the MES and MP churches adopted social creeds with very similar wording in the 1910s, and in some form this statement has been included in every Methodist *Discipline* since that time. The CME Church adopted a Social Creed and has expanded it over the years into a chapter of their *Discipline*. At the time of its formation in 1946, the EUB Church also adopted a statement of social concern. Although differences in wording exist between various versions of the Social Creed, the Methodist family has asserted a strong consensus in social concerns through it. The Social Creed stands as another indication that for Methodist churches, many moral issues have the status of the formal doctrines expressed in our more historic confessions.

★ ★ ★

We have stated at the beginning of this chapter that some aspects of the historic Methodist ethos may seem quaint today. One could make the case, though, that observance of the Lord's Day as a day of rest and quiet (just to take one instance) might make for a better world. Sometimes Methodists have divided within themselves over which issues to take most seriously. Evangelically oriented Methodists tend to stress personal morality, including abstinence from alcohol and tobacco and the need for sexual purity. Socially progressive Methodists have often stressed the need for social transformation and involvement in more systemic issues such as the abolition of slavery or the rights of children and women. In a world that often seems to lack moral bearings, though, it may be important to stress the wholeness and balance of the historic Methodist moral vision, a vision that insists that both the individual and society must be transformed by divine grace.

Resources and References: The quotation from C. S. Lewis is from *Mere Christianity* (New York: Macmillan, 1960), p. 80. On the use and relevance of the General Rules, see Michael G. Cartwright, "The General Rules *Revisited*" (*Catalyst* 24:4 [April 1998], pp. 1-2). The mission statement of the AME Church is quoted from the denomination's 1992 *Doctrine and Discipline,* p. 13. On the involvement of southern churchwomen in the Civil Rights movement, see Alice G. Knotts, *Fellowship of Love: Methodist Women Changing American Racial Attitudes, 1920–1968* (Nashville: Kingswood Books, 1996).

APPENDIX 1

TEXTS OF THE APOSTLES' CREED, THE TWENTY-FIVE ARTICLES OF RELIGION, AND THE GENERAL RULES

Note: This appendix gives the complete texts for three doctrinal standards held in common by the AME, AMEZ, CME, and UM churches. Some differences in wording among these churches are noted in brackets.

The Apostles' Creed

I believe in God the Father Almighty, maker of heaven and earth.

And in Jesus Christ his only Son our Lord: who was conceived by the Holy Spirit, born of the Virgin Mary, suffered under Pontius Pilate, was crucified, dead and buried;[†] the third day he rose from the dead; he ascended into heaven, and sitteth at the right hand of God the Father Almighty; from thence he shall come to judge the quick and the dead.

I believe in the Holy Spirit, the holy catholic church, the communion of saints, the forgiveness of sins, the resurrection of the body, and the life everlasting. Amen.

Note: †The ecumenical use of this creed includes the words "he descended into hell" at this point. Nineteenth-century Methodists objected to the thought that Christ went to "hell" as the place of judgment, which was not the intended meaning of the creed. Dialogue with other churches has encouraged Methodists to restore the creed to its ecumenical form (cf. UM Hymnal [1989], no. 882; see chapter 2).

Twenty-five Articles of Religion (1784)

Note: The Twenty-five Articles of Religion are shared by the AME, AMEZ, CME, and UM churches. There are some differences in the texts of the Articles received by these churches. Most of these are simply differences in punctuation or differences resulting from attempts to modernize the antiquated language of the Articles, and I have not noted such minor differences. In a few cases there are somewhat more significant alterations or omissions that have been noted. The following text is based on a comparison of the texts as given in the most recent *Disciplines* of these four denominations.

1. Of Faith in the Holy Trinity

There is but one living and true God, everlasting, without body or parts, of infinite power, wisdom, and goodness; the maker and preserver of all things, both visible and invisible. And in unity of this Godhead there are three persons, of one substance, power, and eternity—the Father, the Son, and the Holy Ghost.

2. Of the Word, or Son of God, Who Was Made Very Man

The Son, who is the Word of the Father, the very and eternal God, of one substance with the Father, took man's nature in the womb of the blessed Virgin; so that two whole and perfect natures—that is to say, the Godhead and manhood—were joined together in one person, never to be divided; whereof is one Christ, very God and very man, who truly suffered, was crucified, dead and buried to reconcile his Father to us, and to be a sacrifice, not only for original guilt, but also for [the] actual sins of men.

3. Of the Resurrection of Christ

Christ did truly rise again from the dead, and took again his body, with all things appertaining to the perfection of human nature, wherewith he ascended into heaven, and there sitteth until he return to judge all men at the last day.

4. Of the Holy Ghost

The Holy Ghost, proceeding from the Father and the Son, is of one substance, majesty, and glory with the Father and the Son, very and eternal God.

5. Of the Sufficiency
of the Holy Scriptures for Salvation

The Holy Scripture containeth all things necessary to salvation; so that whatsoever is not read therein, nor may be proved thereby, is not to be required of any man that it should be believed as an article of faith, or be thought requisite or necessary to salvation. In the name of the Holy Scripture we do understand those canonical books of the Old and New Testament of whose authority was never any doubt in the church. The names of the canonical books are:

Genesis, Exodus, Leviticus, Numbers, Deuteronomy, Joshua, Judges, Ruth, The First Book of Samuel, The Second Book of Samuel, The First Book of Kings, The Second Book of Kings, The First Book of Chronicles, The Second Book of Chronicles, The Book of Ezra, The Book of Nehemiah, The Book of Esther, The Book of Job, The Psalms, The Proverbs, Ecclesiastes or the Preacher, Cantica or Songs of Solomon, Four Prophets the Greater, Twelve Prophets the Less.

All the books of the New Testament, as they are commonly received, we do receive and account canonical.

6. Of the Old Testament

The Old Testament is not contrary to the New; for both in the Old and New Testament everlasting life is offered to mankind by Christ, who is the only Mediator between God and man, being both God and man. Wherefore they are not to be heard who feign that the old fathers did look only for transitory promises. Although the law given from God by Moses, as touching ceremonies and rites, doth not bind Christians, nor ought the civil precepts thereof of necessity be received in any commonwealth; yet, notwithstanding, no Christian whatsoever is free from the obedience of the commandments which are called moral.

7. Of Original or Birth Sin

Original sin standeth not in the following [CME: "falling"] of Adam (as the Pelagians do vainly talk [AME: "say"]), but it is the corruption of the nature of every man, that naturally is engendered of the offspring of Adam, whereby man is very far gone from original righteousness, and of his own nature inclined to evil, and that continually.

8. Of Free Will

The condition of man after the fall of Adam is such that he cannot turn and prepare himself, by his own natural strength and works, to faith, and calling upon God; wherefore we have no power to do good works, pleasant and acceptable to God, without the grace of God by Christ preventing [AME: "assisting"] us, that we may have a good will, and working with us, when we have that good will.

9. Of the Justification of Man

We are accounted righteous before God only for the merit of our Lord and Saviour Jesus Christ, by faith, and not for our own works or deservings. Wherefore, that we are justified by faith, only, is a most wholesome doctrine, and very full of comfort.

10. Of Good Works

Although good works, which are the fruits of faith, and follow after justification, cannot put away our sins, and endure the severity of God's judgments; yet are they pleasing and acceptable to God in Christ and spring out of a true and lively faith insomuch that by them a lively faith may be as evidently known as a tree is discerned by its fruit.

11. Of Works of Supererogation

Voluntary works—besides, over, and above God's commandments—which are called [UM and AME: "they call"] works of supererogation, cannot be taught without arrogancy and impiety. For by them men do declare that they do not only render unto God as much as they are bound to do, but that they do more for his sake than of bounden duty is required: whereas Christ saith plainly; When ye [UM: "you"] have done all that is commanded you, say, We are unprofitable servants.

12. Of Sin After Justification

Not every sin willingly committed after justification is the sin against the Holy Ghost, and unpardonable. Wherefore, the grant of repentance is not to be denied to such as fall into sin after justification. After we have received the Holy Ghost, we may depart from grace given, and fall into sin, and, by the grace of God, rise again and amend our lives. And therefore they are to be condemned who say they can no more sin as long as they live here; or deny the place of forgiveness to such as truly repent.

13. Of the Church

The visible Church of Christ is a congregation of faithful men, in which the pure Word of God is preached, and the Sacraments duly administered according to Christ's ordinance, in all those things that of necessity are requisite to the same.

14. Of Purgatory

The Romish doctrine concerning purgatory, pardon, worshiping, and adoration, as well of images as of relics, and also invocation of saints, is a fond thing, vainly invented, and grounded upon no warrant of Scripture, but repugnant to the Word of God.

15. Of Speaking in the Congregation in Such a Tongue as the People Understand

It is a thing plainly repugnant to the Word of God, and the custom of the primitive church, to have public prayer in the church, or to minister the Sacraments, in a tongue not understood by the people.

16. Of the Sacraments

Sacraments ordained of Christ are not only badges of Christian men's profession, but rather they are certain signs of grace, and God's good will toward us, by the which he doth work invisibly in us, and doth not only quicken, but also strengthen and confirm our faith in him.

There are two sacraments ordained of Christ our Lord in the Gospel; that is to say, Baptism and the Supper of the Lord.

Those five commonly called sacraments, that is to say, confirmation, penance, orders, matrimony, and extreme unction, are not to be counted for Sacraments of the Gospel; being such as have partly grown out of the corrupt following of the apostles, and partly are states of life allowed in the Scriptures, but yet have not the like nature of Baptism and the Lord's Supper, because they have not any visible sign or ceremony ordained of God.

The sacraments were not ordained of Christ to be gazed upon, or to be carried about; but that we should duly use them. And in such only as worthily receive the same they have a wholesome effect or operation; but they that receive them unworthily, purchase to themselves condemnation, as St. Paul saith, [1 Cor. xi. 29].

[Omitted in AME and UM]

17. Of Baptism

Baptism is not only a sign of profession, and mark of difference [whereby Christians are distinguished from others that are not baptized]; but it is also a sign of regeneration or [AME "of"] the new birth. The baptism of young children is to be retained in the Church.

[Omitted in AME]

18. Of the Lord's Supper

The Supper of the Lord is not only a sign of the love that Christians ought to have among themselves one to another, but rather is a sacrament of our redemption by Christ's death; insomuch that, to such as rightly, worthily, and with faith receive the same, the bread which we break is a partaking of the body of Christ; and likewise the cup of blessing is a partaking of the blood of Christ.

Transubstantiation, or the change of the substance of bread and wine in the Supper of our Lord, cannot be proved by Holy Writ, but is repugnant to the plain words of Scripture, overthroweth the nature of a sacrament, and hath given occasion to many superstitions.

The body of Christ is given, taken, and eaten in the Supper, only after a heavenly and spiritual manner. And the mean whereby the body of Christ is received and eaten in the Supper is faith.

The Sacrament of the Lord's Supper was not by Christ's ordinance reserved, carried about, lifted up, or worshiped.

19. Of Both Kinds

The cup of the Lord is not to be denied to the lay people; for both the parts of the Lord's Supper, by Christ's ordinance and commandment, ought to be administered to all Christians alike.

20. Of the One Oblation of Christ, Finished upon the Cross

The offering of Christ, once made, is that [AMEZ "a"] perfect redemption, propitiation and satisfaction for all the sins of the whole world, both original and actual; and there is none other satisfaction for sin but that alone. Wherefore the sacrifice [AME "sacraments"] of masses, in the which it is commonly said that the priest doth offer Christ for the quick and the dead, to have remission of pain or guilt, is a blasphemous fable and dangerous deceit.

21. Of the Marriage of Ministers

The ministers of Christ are not commanded by God's law either to vow the estate of single life or to abstain from marriage; therefore it is lawful for them, as for all other Christians, to marry at their own discretion, as they shall judge the same to serve best [AME "better"] to godliness.

22. Of the Rites and Ceremonies of Churches

It is not necessary that rites and ceremonies should in all places be the same, or exactly alike;

for they have been always different, and may be changed according to the diversity of countries, times, and men's manners, so that nothing be ordained against God's Word. Whosoever, through his private judgment willingly and purposely doth openly break the rites and ceremonies of the church to which he belongs, which are not [AMEZ and CME omit "not"] repugnant to the Word of God, and are [AMEZ adds "not"] ordained and approved by common authority, ought to be rebuked openly, that others may fear to do the like, as one that offendeth against the common order of the church, and woundeth the consciences of weak brethren.

Every particular church may ordain, change, or abolish rites and ceremonies, so that all things may be done to edification.

23. Of the Rulers of the United States of America

The President, the Congress, the general assemblies, the Governors, and the councils of state, *as the delegates of the people,* are the rulers of the United States of America, according to the division of power made to them by the [Constitution of the United States, and by the] constitutions of their respective states. And the said states are a sovereign and independent nation, and ought not to be subject to any foreign jurisdiction.

[Omitted in CME]

[AMEZ adds a section relevant to persons not in the USA]

24. Of Christian Men's Goods

The riches and goods of Christians are not common as touching the right, title, and possession

of the same, as some do falsely boast. Notwithstanding, every man ought, of such things as he
possesseth, liberally to give alms to the poor,
according to his ability.

25. Of a Christian Man's Oath

As we confess that vain and rash swearing is forbidden Christian men by our Lord Jesus Christ
and James his apostle, so we judge that the Christian religion doth not prohibit but that a man may
swear when the magistrate requireth, in a cause
of faith and charity, so it be done according to the
prophet's teaching, in justice, judgment, and
truth.

The General Rules (1743; revised)

The Nature, Design, and General Rules
of Our United Societies

[Preface
Omitted in
CME *Dis-
cipline*]

In the latter end of the year 1739 eight or ten
persons came to Mr. Wesley, in London, who
appeared to be deeply convinced of sin, and
earnestly groaning for redemption. They desired,
as did two or three more the next day, that he
would spend some time with them in prayer, and
advise them how to flee from the wrath to come,
which they saw continually hanging over their
heads. That he might have more time for this
great work, he appointed a day when they might
all come together, which from thenceforward
they did every week, namely, on Thursday in the
evening. To these, and as many more as desired
to join with them (for their number increased
daily), he gave those advices from time to time

which he judged most needful for them, and they always concluded their meeting with prayer suited to their several necessities.

This was the rise of the *United Society,* first in Europe, and then in America. Such a society is no other than "a company of men having the form and seeking the power of godliness, united in order to pray together, to receive the word of exhortation, and to watch over one another in love, that they may help each other to work out their salvation."

That it may the more easily be discerned whether they are indeed working out their own salvation, each society is divided into smaller companies, called *classes,* according to their respective places of abode. There are about twelve [AMEZ: "to thirty"] persons in a class, one of whom is styled the *leader.* It is his duty:

1. To see each person in his class once a week at least, in order: (1) to inquire how their souls prosper; (2) to advise, reprove, comfort or exhort, as occasion may require; (3) to receive what they are willing to give toward the relief of the preachers, church, and poor.

2. To meet the ministers [AMEZ: "Preacher"] and the stewards of the society once a week [AMEZ: "month"], in order: (1) to inform the minister of any that are sick, or of any that walk disorderly and will not be reproved; (2) to pay the stewards what they have received of their several classes in the week [AMEZ: "month"] preceding.

[CME Begins Here] There is only one condition previously required of those who desire admission into these societies: "a desire to flee from the wrath to come, and to be saved from their sins." But wherever this is really fixed in the soul it will be shown by its fruits.

It is therefore expected of all who continue therein that they should continue to evidence their desire of salvation,

First: By doing no harm, by avoiding evil of every kind, especially that which is most generally practiced, such as:

The taking of the name of God in vain.

The profaning the day of the Lord, either by doing ordinary work therein or by buying or selling.

Drunkenness: buying or selling [CME: "or drinking"; AME: "or the drinking of"; AMEZ: "or using"] spirituous liquors, [UMC: "or drinking them"] unless in cases of [UMC: "extreme"] necessity.

[AME and CME Omit] Slaveholding; buying or selling slaves.

[AME: "The buying and selling of men, women and children with an intention to enslave them."]

Fighting, quarreling, brawling, brother going to law with brother; returning evil for evil, or railing for railing; the using many words in buying or selling.

The buying or selling goods that have not paid the duty.

The giving or taking things on usury i.e., unlawful interest.

Uncharitable or unprofitable conversation; particularly speaking evil of magistrates or of ministers.

Doing to others as we would not they should do unto us.

Doing what we know is not for the glory of God, as:

The putting on of gold and costly apparel [AMEZ: "as a useless ornament"]

The taking such diversions as cannot be used in the name of the Lord Jesus [AMEZ: "such as dancing, card-playing, lottery, policy, and other games of chance, going to circuses and theatres"].

The singing those songs, or reading those books, which do not tend to the knowledge or love of God.

Softness and needless self-indulgence.

Laying up treasure upon earth.

Borrowing without a probability of paying; or taking up goods without a probability of paying for them.

It is expected of all who continue in these societies that they should continue to evidence their desire of salvation,

Secondly: By doing good; by being in every kind merciful after their power; as they have opportunity, doing good of every possible sort, and, as far as possible, to all men:

To their bodies, of the ability which God giveth, by giving food to the hungry, by clothing the naked, by visiting or helping them that are sick or in prison.

To their souls, by instructing, reproving, or exhorting all we have any intercourse with; trampling under foot that enthusiastic doctrine that "we are not to do good unless our hearts be free to it."

By doing good, especially to them that are of the household of faith or groaning so to be; employing them preferably to others; buying one of another, helping each other in business, and so much the more because the world will love its own and them only.

By all possible diligence and frugality, that the gospel be not blamed.

By running with patience the race which is set before them, denying themselves, and taking up their cross daily; submitting to bear the reproach of Christ, to be as the filth and offscouring of the world; and looking that men should say all manner of evil of them falsely, for the Lord's sake.

It is expected of all who desire to continue in these societies that they should continue to evidence their desire of salvation,

Thirdly: By attending upon all the ordinances of God; such are:

The public worship of God.

The ministry of the Word, either read or expounded [AMEZ: "explained"].

The Supper of the Lord.

Family and private prayer.   [AME Puts Last]

Searching the Scriptures.

Fasting or abstinence.

These are the General Rules of our societies; all of which we are taught of God to observe, even in his written Word, which is the only rule, and the sufficient rule, both of our faith and practice. And all these we know his Spirit writes on truly awakened hearts. If there be any among us who observe them not, who habitually break any of them, let it be known unto them who watch over that soul as they who must give an account. We will admonish him of the error of his ways. We will bear with him for a season. But then, if he repent not, he hath no more place among us. We have delivered our own souls.

APPENDIX 2

BACKGROUND NOTES ON HISTORIC METHODIST DOCTRINAL STATEMENTS

Twenty-five Articles of Religion

1. **The Twenty-five Articles of Religion** (AME, AMEZ, CME, UMC). The AME, AMEZ, CME, and UM churches inherited from the Methodist Episcopal Church and its successors Twenty-five Articles of Religion. These were based on Twenty-four Articles which John Wesley edited from the Thirty-nine Articles of the Church of England. The Christmas Conference which organized the ME Church in 1784 added another Article "Of the Rulers of the United States of America," making the total twenty-five. In the pattern typical of Protestant doctrinal statements, the Articles deal with issues of trinitarian theology and Christology, the grounds of religious authority, issues of human nature and salvation, and issues of sacramental theology and practice. Since 1808 the Articles have been protected by a Restrictive Rule in the denominations' constitutions in their *Disciplines* and have never been altered except in minor ways noted in appendix 1.

General Rules

2. **The General Rules** (AME, AMEZ, CME, UMC). The "General Rules" were drawn up by John Wesley in 1743 and functioned as a kind of contract by which members of early Methodist Societies agreed to hold each other accountable for specific moral behaviors (under the three categories of "doing good of all kinds," "avoiding evil of all kinds," and "attending upon the ordinances of God"). These have been protected by a Restrictive Rule since 1808, and up until 1939 all ME and MES elders were required to read the General Rules to their congregations once annually. The prohibition against slaveholding and slave trade in the General Rules was the grounds for the most significant division in the Methodist Episcopal Church (1844), but because the General Rules are concerned with issues generally appropriate to eighteenth-century Britain (such as avoiding goods that have not paid import tariffs), they have not been consistently utilized by Methodists in this century. The AMEZ Church has made the most significant alterations to the text of the General Rules (see chapter 7). Their revisions indicate how seriously this document was taken by Zion Methodists. We might note, further, that in the AME *Discipline*, the General Rules are followed by Wesley's "Rules of Band Societies" and "Rules for Giving."

General Rules

3. **Catechism on Faith** (AME). A revision of Wesley's "Doctrinal Minutes" is included in AME *Disciplines* from 1817 (the first AME *Discipline*) through the present as Section II, following the Articles of Religion, and they form a catechism of distinctly Methodist doctrine. The "Doctrinal Minutes" were a collation of minutes

AME Catechism on Faith

of the earliest Methodist Annual Conferences (1744–1748), and were in effect the original charter of Methodism (the "United Societies") as a religious movement within the Church of England. They deal with the doctrines of repentance, faith, justification, assurance, sanctification, and the role of the Methodist community as a means of grace.

AME Statement on Apostolic Succession and Religious Formalism

4. **Statement on "Apostolic Succession" and "Religious Formalism"** (AME). A number of persons associated with the Free African Society and the early AME Church, including Absalom Jones, became Episcopalians, and there was a consistent fear of Episcopalian concerns about the doctrine of "apostolic succession" and the general "formalism" that African Methodists perceived on the part of Anglicans. A motion to adopt new doctrinal statements on "Apostolic Succession and Religious Formalism" was adopted by the 1884 General Conference of the AME Church, meeting in Baltimore, in response to claims that apostolic succession is necessary to the true existence of the church. The statement has been reprinted in all AME *Disciplines* since that time.

UMC Confession of Faith

5. **Confession of Faith** (UMC). Phillip William Otterbein's successors in the United Brethren in Christ adopted a brief doctrinal statement in 1816 that was revised numerous times subsequently. The Confession, like the Articles of Religion, deals with issues of trinitarian theology and Christology, grounds of religious authority, human nature and salvation, and sacramental theology and practice. This "Confession of Faith" was inherited by the United Methodist Church

upon its union in 1968, and placed alongside the Articles of Religion. The denomination's new constitution protected the Confession of Faith in the same manner in which the Articles of Religion had been protected in the past.

6. **John Wesley's** *Standard Sermons* (UMC; constitutional status in other churches is unclear). John Wesley's "Model Deed" for Methodist chapels stipulated that preachers in the chapels could not express doctrine at variance with those expressed in the first four volumes of his *Sermons on Several Occasions* and in his *Explanatory Notes upon the New Testament* (see below). This deed was utilized by British Methodists, who still regard the "Wesleyan Standards" (*Sermons* and *Notes*) as their formal doctrinal statements, and by early American Methodists at least until the time of the Christmas Conference (1784). One of the disputed points of American Methodist history is whether the founders of the Methodist Episcopal Church presupposed the Wesleyan Standards, which they failed to name in their earliest *Disciplines,* and whether the Restrictive Rules adopted in 1808 presupposed that the Wesleyan Standards were constitutionally protected along with the Articles of Religion and the General Rules.

Wesley's Standard Sermons

Although Methodists had consistent reference to Wesley's *Sermons* through the nineteenth century, it is unclear whether they functioned as doctrinal standards. At the time of the adoption of "Our Theological Task" (see below) in 1972, the UMC Judicial Council ruled that the Wesleyan

Standards were constitutionally protected. This decision was challenged on the basis of historical scholarship. At the time of a revision of "Our Theological Task" in 1988, the UM General Conference adopted legislation clarifying that the Wesleyan Standards should be understood as part of the doctrinal standards protected by the Restrictive Rules of the Constitution. Although the number of Wesley's sermons constituting a doctrinal standard has been disputed by British and American Methodists, the *Sermons* bear particular importance in laying out the distinctly Wesleyan understanding of the "way of salvation" that lies at the basis of Wesleyan spirituality.

Wesley's *Notes on the New Testament*

7. **John Wesley's *Explanatory Notes upon the New Testament*** (UMC; constitutional status in other churches is unclear). What has been said above about the Wesleyan Standards applies formally to Wesley's *Notes*, although it is relevant to consider that Wesley's *Notes* have been utilized far less frequently than the *Sermons* in Methodist theological reflection. This is because (1) Adam Clarke's *Commentary* replaced Wesley's *Notes* early in the nineteenth century as the favored biblical commentary used by Methodists, and (2) Wesley's biblical scholarship, though progressive for the eighteenth century, seems quite antiquated since the developments of mid-nineteenth-century biblical scholarship.

Social Creed

8. **The Methodist Social Creed** (CME, UMC). The ME Church adopted a Social Creed in 1908 in response to concerns about conditions of workers and urban poverty. This document was revised

slightly and adopted by the MES and MP churches in 1914 and 1916, respectively. A statement of Christian social concern was included in the *Discipline* of the EUB Church at the time of its union in 1946. A Social Creed with similar wording was adopted by the CME Church and has been revised and expanded. Although these creeds do not have the constitutionally protected status of older doctrinal statements such as the Articles of Religion, they complement the General Rules by giving a more contemporary Methodist consensus on social issues.

9. **Statement of "Our Theological Task"** (UMC, not constitutionally protected). The Theological Study Commission established by the 1968 Uniting Conference of the UMC was to have produced a new and reconciled theological statement incorporating the teachings of the Articles of Religion and the Confession of Faith. The Commission chose, instead, to leave the two historical doctrinal statements in place and to adopt in addition to them a contemporary theological statement, interpreting the Wesleyan tradition in the light of contemporary (including ecumenical) issues. Their new statement, which included the first official assertion of the so-called "Wesleyan Quadrilateral" (the use of Scripture, tradition, reason, and experience in theological reflection), was adopted by the General Conference of 1972 with little opposition, but in a surprise move the Judicial Council determined that the new doctrinal statement was to be considered simple legislation (amenable by a simple majority of the General Conference), and not a constitutionally

UM Statement of "Our Theological Task"

protected doctrinal statement as Outler and members of the Commission had intended. This has proved to be a helpful theological document in Methodist theological reflection, and was revised by the General Conference of 1988 to make clear the "primacy" or priority of Scripture among the elements of the Quadrilateral and to make clear Methodist commitment to ecumenical and "apostolic faith" underlying all of our doctrinal statements.

GLOSSARY AND INDEX

The following list serves as an index, glossary, and table of frequently used abbreviations. References are to page numbers in this book. Entries do not always contain glossary definitions; these are given only when I have judged that terms may not be broadly understood.

Annual Conference: The Methodist **Conference** of clergy and lay delegates which meets annually; also, a geographical subdivision of a Methodist denomination's **General (AME, AMEZ, CME)** or **Jurisdictional (UMC) Conference** . . . 18

Apostles' Creed: A creed based on ancient Western (Latin) baptismal creeds, the present form of the Apostles' Creed can be dated only from the Middle Ages (ca. ninth century). It is the most widely used creed in Methodist churches; text given in appendix 1 . . . . 22, 25, 43-44, 81, 100

Apostolic, Apostolicity: Faithfulness to and continuity with the church founded by the apostles; one of the four **notes of the church** 66

Apostolic Succession: Belief rejected by Methodists which maintains that a sign of the true church is the maintenance of an unbroken succession of **bishops** in (or at least from) churches founded by the apostles 38, 68-69

Arianism: Belief rejected in historic Christian faith according to which Christ is a created and temporal (not eternal) being, subordinate to God the Father; the doctrine of the **Trinity** expressed in the **Nicene Creed** was formulated in response to Arianism in the 300s A.D. 41-42

Arminian/Arminianism: Belief favored in Methodist teaching that God intends the salvation of all human beings, that Christ died for all human beings, and that human free will (as a gift of divine grace) is compatible with divine sovereignty 50-51

Articles of Religion: The Twenty-five Articles of Religion are a doctrinal standard for the **AME, AMEZ, CME** and **UM** denominations. They are derived from Twenty-four Articles condensed by **John Wesley** from the Thirty-nine Articles of the **Church of England,** subsequently revised by the **ME** Christmas Conference in 1784. The text is given in appendix 1; notes in appendix 2 . . . . 13, 21, 23, 101-10, 116

Assurance: Historic Methodist teaching maintained that when a person is **justified,** he or she experiences a divinely given assurance of the forgiveness of sins 56-58

Awakening: An experience typical of early Methodist spirituality in which an individual came to an intense awareness of his

Eucharist: see **Lord's Supper.**

Experience: Methodists have been concerned with the religious experience of persons; the so-called **Wesleyan Quadrilateral** acknowledges experience as a way of interpreting Scripture. 39

Faith: According to Methodist doctrine, faith involves more than simply assent (believing *that* certain things are true), it must involve heartfelt trust as well 56

Falling from Grace: Informal term for the Methodist doctrine that an individual may lose **faith** in Christ and so forfeit their **justification;** John Wesley's sermon on "The Wilderness State" describes this possibility; this teaching stands in opposition to the teaching of **eternal security** favored in other Christian traditions 59-60

Fasting: Fasting ("or abstinence") is a spiritual discipline for which the **General Rules** hold Methodists accountable . . . 87

Free Will: Methodist doctrine maintains that as a result of **prevenient** grace, all human beings have the possibility of free consent to God 50, 51

Frequent or Constant Communion: Methodist spiritual teaching from the time of the Wesleys encouraged frequent and regular use of the Lord's Supper, although from the 1800s Methodists became accustomed to infrequent (monthly or quarterly) communion 77

Gambling: Methodists historically opposed all forms of gambling both because of its nature as a worldly **amusement** and its irresponsible use of **money** or resources; see also **stewardship** 92

Gender-Specific Language in Reference to God: The belief that **God** is "without body or parts" (first **Article of Religion)** makes gender-specific language in reference to God problematic despite the fact that traditional language about God has been heavily masculine; Christians are now seeking discernment as to how they can agree on language about God (especially language to describe the **Trinity)** that does not involve the problems of gender-specific language 42-43

General Conference: In the **AME, AMEZ, CME,** and **UM** churches, the General Conference is the highest representative

Human Condition: Methodist doctrine insists that all human beings stand in need of divine **grace;** see also **original sin** 48-50

Human Nature of Christ: Methodist doctrine affirms with historic Christian teaching that Christ had a fully human nature as well as a fully **divine** nature 43-44

Hymns/Hymnals: Methodist doctrine since the time of the **Wesleys** has been expressed and taught in hymns; even the outline of hymnals conveys doctrinal content 24, 53-54, 85

Inclusiveness of the Church: see **Catholicity.**

Infant Baptism: Methodist churches affirm and practice infant baptism on the grounds of household baptisms in the early church, Jesus' invitation to the children, and children's need for the Christian community. 73-74

Itinerancy (or "Itineracy"): "Itinerant" means traveling or moving about from place to place; early Methodist preachers did this quite literally, although since the late 1800s itinerancy has come to denote the distinct Methodist appointive system for **elders** rather than the need for constant travel 68

Judgment: Methodist doctrine affirms with the historic Christian tradition that Christ will come to be our final judge . . . 80-81

Justice Issues: Methodist **social morality** has been concerned with justice issues (see the **Social Creed**) grounded in a concern for the **sanctification** of society. 92-98

Justification, Justifying Grace: Justification is the gracious act of God in restoring human beings to a right relationship with God and thereby forgiving their **sins;** justifying grace is the divine favor and power by which this is accomplished; Methodist doctrine holds that our justification is by grace through faith 56

Kingdom of God: The rule or reign of God, to which Christians look forward 82

Lay Preaching: The Methodist movement has utilized lay preachers since the 1740s; Wesley insisted that lay preachers had an "extraordinary ministry" different from that of **ordained** ministers; Methodist churches have trained and employed lay or "local" preachers, sometimes empowering them as pastors of local congregations to celebrate the **sacraments,** though this custom is not universal 69

prevenient grace is **universally available** and is the ground of human **free will** 54-55

Preventing Grace: see **Prevenient Grace.**

Primacy of Scripture: The teaching upheld in Methodist doctrine according to which the **Bible** has primary authority in the life of the **church** 35-36

Priest: In older Christian traditions (Orthodox, Roman Catholic, and **Anglican**), the second order of **ordained ministry,** whose ministry includes celebration of **baptism** and the **Lord's Supper;** John Wesley was a priest of the **Church of England,** and the Methodist order of **elder** (a literal translation of the Greek *presbyteros*) answers to the order of priest in the older traditions. 66, 67-68

Prohibition: Methodists supported efforts for the prohibition of **alcoholic** beverages as a social extension of their concern for **temperance** or **abstinence** 92

Purgatory: The belief rejected in Methodist doctrine according to which the souls of believers in the period between death and the final **judgment** are purified and can be assisted by the prayers of living persons. 81-82

Real Presence: A term favored by many **Anglicans** to describe teachings about the **Lord's Supper** according to which there is a "real" presence of Christ conveyed by the **sacrament,** without specifying whether this presence is **corporeal** or a distinct spiritual power (**virtualism**). 76

Reason: John Wesley believed that human **reason** aided by divine **grace** could assist in interpreting the **Bible;** the **UM** statement of **Our Theological Task** affirms the use of reason along with **tradition** and **experience** as a means of interpreting Scripture; see also the **Wesleyan Quadrilateral** 38-39

Rededication, Renewal: Methodist teaching on **sanctification** calls for consistent rededication or renewal of our relationship to the Savior. 59

Reformed Tradition: The broad Christian tradition associated with Zwingli and Calvin and represented by both Presbyterian and Congregational churches; the **UMC** has roots in the Reformed tradition by way of **Phillip William Otterbein** and the **UB** Church 15, 72-73, 75

Slavery/Slaveholding: Methodist **social morality** included opposition to slavery, and the **ME** Discipline of 1808 specified slaveholding as an evil to be avoided by Methodists. The schism of the **MES** Church from the **ME** Church came about over the issue of slaveholding 16, 94-95

Social Morality: Methodist social morality included active involvement in social reform and even political action designed to alleviate social conditions; for Methodists, this was seen as one aspect of the **sanctification** of the world 60, 92-98

Speech: Methodist **personal morality** was concerned with issues of speech, urging believers to speak reverently of **God** and respectfully of other persons 89

Steward: A permanent lay office in Methodist churches; Methodist stewards (discontinued in the **UMC**) have ongoing responsibility for the oversight of their congregations' ministries. 70

Stewardship: Careful and responsible use of the blessings **God** has given us; Methodists encourage careful stewardship of **money** and other possessions 90-91

Sufficiency of Scripture: The Methodist teaching (inherited from the **Church of England**) which maintains that the **Bible** contains everything we need to know for salvation. 35-36

Sunday: see **Lord's Day.**

Swearing: Methodist **personal morality** regarding **speech** ruled out swearing as inappropriate and irreverent 89

Temperance: Methodists recognized the danger of **alcoholic** beverages early on and encouraged temperance; growing recognition of alcohol-related problems caused Methodists eventually to advocate total **abstinence** from alcohol. 91-92

Tradition: That which we value from the past; Methodist teachings on religious authority acknowledge the value of Christian tradition as a means of interpreting the **Bible;** see also **Wesleyan Quadrilateral.** 37-38

Transubstantiation: Roman Catholic teaching concerning the **Lord's Supper** rejected in Methodist Articles and UM Confession according to which the inner reality of bread and wine are replaced with Christ's body and blood; not to be confused with **corporeal presence;** see also **real presence, virtualism,** and

Way of Salvation: The process of salvation from the beginnings of God's work under **prevenient grace** through **justification** and **sanctification** expressed in historic Methodist doctrinal statements (including Wesley's *Sermons*) and in the structure of Methodist **hymnals** 20, 24, 48, 53-54, 62-63

WCC World Council of Churches: Ecumenical organization in which the **Pan-Methodist** churches all participate; the WCC's Faith and Order Commission has developed a number of consensus documents including **BEM** 26, 41, 67, 74

Wesley, Charles (1707-1788): Anglican priest, the brother of **John Wesley,** who contributed thousands of **hymns** explicating Methodist spiritual and social teachings 54

Wesley, John (1703-1791): Anglican priest, the brother of **Charles Wesley,** who founded the Methodist movement within in the **Church of England** 19, 25, 53, 54

Wesleyan Quadrilateral: The use of the **Bible, tradition, reason,** and **experience** as a method for theological reflection; although John Wesley himself did not lay out the Quadrilateral as such, he did use these four authorities; the Wesleyan Quadrilateral was first expressed in the **UM** statement of **Our Theological Task** 39-40

WMC World Methodist Council: International body representing global Methodism. The **AME, AMEZ, CME,** and **UM** Churches and their predecessors have been members of the **WMC** since its founding in 1881 . . . . 13, 16

Worship: The expression of ultimate or final valuing; public worship is enjoined upon Methodists as an "ordinance of God" in the **General Rules** 41-42, 46-47, 86-87

Zwinglianism: see **Memorialism.**